DESIGN EDUCATION AND CURRICULUM PLANNING

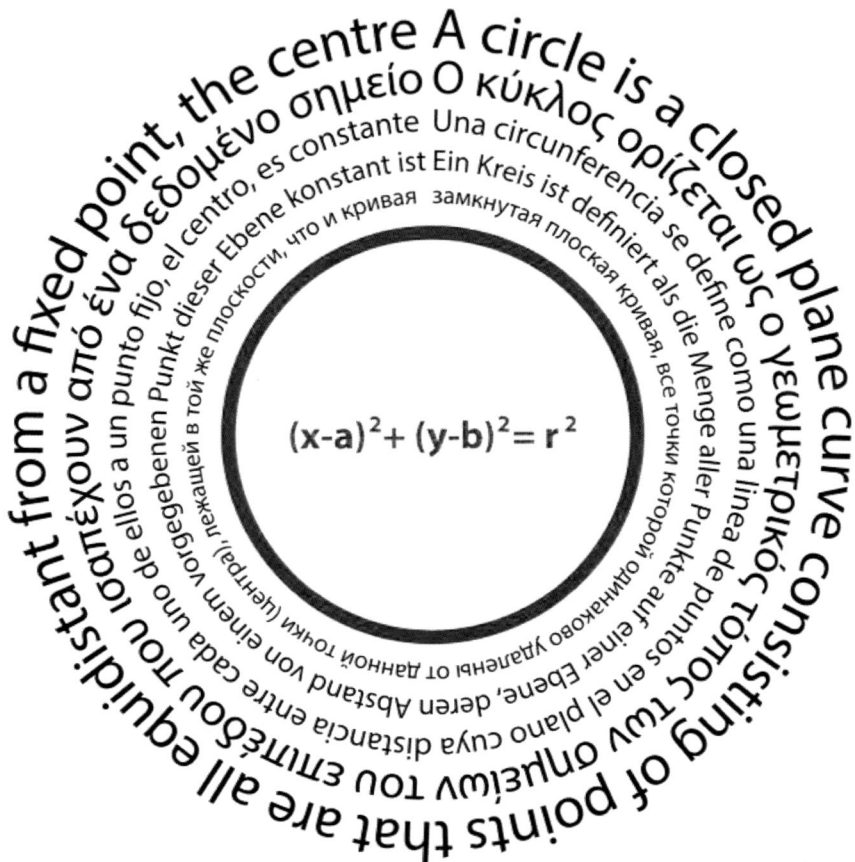

Figure 1 Defining a circle using literacy, numeracy and graphicacy (... in English, Greek, Spanish, German and Russian in the decreasing diameter concentric circles).

[Originally Figure 1.7 in Danos, 2014: 58]

DESIGN EDUCATION AND CURRICULUM PLANNING

Edited by Eddie Norman and Ken Baynes

Published by: Loughborough Design Press Ltd, 6 Mulberry Way, Rothley, Leicestershire, LE7 7TX

Copyright for this edition © 2017, Loughborough Design Press

All rights reserved. Extracts from the book may be reproduced for academic purposes, otherwise written permission is required from the publisher. The book is sold subject to the condition that it shall not by way of trade or otherwise be stored in a retrieval system, re-sold, hired out or otherwise circulated except in the publisher's binding.

For information on all Loughborough Design Press publications, please visit our website: www.ldpress.co.uk

Printed by Printondemand-worldwide.com, UK
The paperback is FSC and PEFC certified

ISBN: [paperback] 978-1-909671-15-7
eISBN: [ePub] 978-1-909671-16-4
eISBN: [mobi] 978-1-909671-17-1

PEFC Certified

This product is from sustainably managed forests and controlled sources

www.pefc.org

Mixed Sources
Product group from well-managed forests, and other controlled sources
www.fsc.org Cert no. TT-COC-002641
© 1996 Forest Stewardship Council

ACKNOWLEDGEMENTS

We would like to thank the Design and Technology Association for permission to reproduce the Editorial from Issue 18.2 of *Design and Technology Education: an international journal* 'Design Epistemology and Curriculum Planning', which was published in June 2013. We are also very grateful to our contributors who made space in their diaries in order to contribute to this initial short volume. We very much hope that this will be the start of an intriguing and important journey for us all.

Book and cover design: Eddie Norman

CONTENTS

1. INTRODUCTION — 6

2. FIRST THOUGHTS ON DESIGN EPISTEMOLOGY
   Eddie Norman

3. OTHERS' FIRST THOUGHTS ON DESIGN EPISTEMOLOGY — 9

   3.1 SO WHAT WENT WRONG AND WHY? — 13
   Stephanie Atkinson

   3.2 HOW DID THE EXPERT PANEL CONCLUDE THAT D&T SHOULD BE MOVED TO A BASIC CURRICULUM? — 18
   Alison Hardy

   3.3 SOME THOUGHTS ON LOCATING DESIGN KNOWLEDGE — 22
   Steve Keirl

   3.4 HOW WE KNOW, WHAT WE SHOULD KNOW: THE BUILDING BLOCKS OF CULTURAL AWARENESS IN DESIGN EDUCATION — 28
   Graham Newman

   3.5 KNOWLEDGE BY DESIGN — 32
   Tristram Shepard

   3.6 DESIGN THINKING: WHAT IS IT AND WHERE MIGHT IT RESIDE? — 39
   David Spendlove

4. EPISTEMOLOGY AND VISUAL THINKING — 43

   4.1 MEANING WITHOUT WORDS — 47
   Ken Baynes

   4.2 GRAPHICACY AND A TAXONOMY — 64
   Xenia Danos

5. DESIGN EPISTEMOLOGY: A WIDER PERSPECTIVE? — 85
   Ken Baynes

6. MAKING FURTHER PROGRESS — 93
   Eddie Norman & Ken Baynes

   AUTHOR PROFILES — 101

1. INTRODUCTION

This short volume has been published to explore an apparently on-going gap in the discourse surrounding design education: the nature of design epistemology, or 'What designers know and how they know it', adapting Vincenti's title (1990). This is in no sense a vocational matter. It is an exploration of alternative ways of knowing, and consequently has profound implications for general education. However, within the currently turbulent times it is the 'vocational' that has the attention of politicians and policymakers, so a vocational perspective has been chosen as the starting point of what is essentially a philosophical discussion. A 'designerly way of knowing' is not an imaginary academic construct, but an everyday reality that requires appropriate consideration and weight in curriculum planning. The failure to acknowledge its importance is a measure of the limited understanding of the curriculum planners.

So, where to begin? Anna Rylander's paper written in 2009 is an exploration from the perspective of management researchers, but begins to get to the heart of the matter. Consider the abstract:

> 'This paper argues that knowledge work and design thinking represent different approaches to problem-solving based on fundamentally different epistemologies: a rational, analytic – or "intellectual" – approach, versus an interpretive, emergent, and explicitly embodied approach. While problems to be addressed may be of similar, overlapping, or completely different character, knowledge-intensive firms and design firms have different perspectives for framing problems and different processes and resources at their disposal for solving problems. By comparing the two perspectives on problem-solving and highlighting their different epistemological roots and research traditions gaps where the two perspectives could cross-fertilize each other, for researchers as well as practitioners, are revealed.' (2009: 1)

Within the knowledge-based economy two different approaches are being acknowledged: the 'intellectual' and what has become known as 'design thinking', which is 'interpretative, emergent and explicitly embodied'. Perhaps inevitably given the current level of understanding of design epistemology, the nature and meaning of 'design thinking' is much contested, but the key point here is that 'knowledge-intensive firms and design firms have different perspectives for framing problems'. All these organizations make vital contributions to the economy and, simply taking a vocational perspective, education should enable people to develop capabilities to contribute to both the rational, analytic or 'intellectual' approach and to approaches that are 'interpretative, emergent and explicitly embodied'. And, of course, this is much more than a vocational matter. This is about everyone in their everyday lives, as well as the knowledge-based economy.

So, how can such an important area be so neglected? This is one of the key questions that this book must explore, but perhaps part of the answer lies with the term 'design thinking'. If the exponents of such approaches instead referred to 'designerly ways of thinking and knowing', then perhaps the idea that design did not have a distinct epistemology would not have taken ground. There might at least be acknowledgement that there are designerly ways of knowing, even if they were not well understood. However, perhaps the major obstacle to progress is that design epistemology must embody the visual. Consider this passage from Anna Rylander's paper:

> Three "types of knowledge" characterize design according to Utterback et al. (2006): knowledge about technological opportunities, about user needs, and about product languages (i.e. the signs that can be used to deliver a message to the user and the cultural context in which the user will give meaning to those signs). Most importantly, however, is the balance between those types of knowledge, and the ability to *integrate* them.
>
> As opposed to "knowledge workers," who typically have a business or engineering degree, designers are predominantly trained in art schools, where processes of knowledge creation are marked by interaction with visual and physical elements as well as with words and numbers. Design schools characteristically use design studios as their central educational device. In a process of learning by doing, students are set a series of design problems to solve. They learn how to design largely by "doing" rather than by studying and analyzing (Lawson, 2006). Drawing and sketching constitute an essential part of the knowledge creation process. Designers learn to "think with their hands" (Collopy, 2004), using sketches, prototypes, and intuition to arrive at their final solutions. Schön (1983) described this process as "having a conversation" with the drawing. Design as problem-solving is thus embodied in character and requires the ability to embrace many different kinds of thought and knowledge - art, science, and technology. Design solutions therefore tend to be holistic, and designers have been referred to as "knowledge brokers" (Hargadon & Sutton, 2000).   (2009: 5)

So, what is it that designers learn to do? How do designers think with their hands? What is that designers know when they graduate that enables them to embrace many different kinds of thought and knowledge? How do designers engage 'with visual and physical elements as well as with words and numbers'? What kind of learning experiences enable design students to develop such capability? Well, seeking answers to these and the many related questions is the pathway to understanding the meaning of a 'designerly way of knowing', and hence, design epistemology.

The Editorial that appears in Chapter 2 was written as a reaction to the debate that was happening in 2013 concerning the future of design and technology in the National Curriculum in England and Wales. It has since become clear that design epistemology remains central to discussions concerning design education. It seems equally clear that there appears to have been little progress in articulating the issues and beginning their resolution. So it is time for a closer look.

To begin the exploration, this introduction and the Editorial were sent to some immediate colleagues in order to bring together some 'First Thoughts' from a number of informed people. This was an initial step along a difficult journey and it was hoped it would provide guidance about some of the immediate stumbling blocks and pitfalls.

References

Collopy F (2004) ' "I think with my hands": On balancing the analytical and the intuitive in Designing'. In R. J. Boland & F. Callopy (eds.), *Managing as Designing*, Stanford University Press, Stanford, CA

Danos X (2014) *Graphicacy and Culture: Refocusing on visual learning*, Loughborough Design Press Ltd, Shepshed, Leicestershire

Hargadon A & Sutton R A (2000) 'Building the innovation factory', *Harvard Business Review*, May-June: 157-66

Lawson B (2006) *How Designers Think*, Architectural Press, Oxford

Rylander A (2009), Forthcoming article accessed at http://www.designfakulteten.kth.se/sites/default/files/1.44194Design_thinking_as_knowledge_work_Anna_Rylander_DT.pdf on 15/9/2017, published as 'Design thinking as knowledge work: epistemological foundations and practical implications', *Journal of Design Management,* 4(1), 7-19

Schön D A (1983) *The Reflective Practitioner: How professionals think in action*, Basic Books, New York

Utterback J, Vedin B A, Alvarez E, Ekman S, Sanderson S W, Tether B, & Verganti R (2006) *Design-inspired innovation*, World Scientific Publishing, Singapore

Vincenti W G (1990) *What Engineers Know and How They Know It: Analytical studies from aeronautical history*, The John Hopkins University Press, Baltimore and London

2. FIRST THOUGHTS ON DESIGN EPISTEMOLOGY

The following Editorial was written in June 2013 by Eddie Norman when design epistemology emerged as a key concern in relation to the discussions that were to determine the future place and shape of design and technology in the National Curriculum for England and Wales. It is used here as a starting point for further, and deeper, consideration of what remains a problematic, but ever more important matter for future curriculum planning relating to design education.

Design and Technology Education: An International Journal 18.2

Design Epistemology and Curriculum Planning
Eddie Norman, Emeritus Professor of Design Education, Loughborough University

Dividing a curriculum into subjects is never going to make it easy to develop effective strategies for design education. In the English National Curriculum design appeared in the documentation in two places; in association with technology (as D&T) and art (as A&D), but some have argued that it has not actually appeared in practice in either. Curriculum politics is interesting, but D&T seems to attract more than its fair share of 'special pleading'. A curriculum derived from the lobbying conducted by special interest groups and selective curriculum development projects tends to be something of a patchwork and lacks a core disciplinary strand. When it comes under challenge there is a serious risk of fragmentation and the whole looking rather less than the sum of the parts, and, at least to some extent, that is the position that D&T in the English National Curriculum now finds itself in.

Essentially, at the root of the current dilemmas lies the question: What is the knowledge base of design? It was the perceived weakness of the epistemological basis of D&T by the 'Expert Panel' that was the focus of its critics. There are two commonly held views concerning design epistemology. The first is that the knowledge base of design is unbounded because the nature and scope of design problems is not definable in advance of designing, and the second holds that there is a fixed core of knowledge that enables designing to take place. The first position leads to the recognition of heuristic-thinking and values that reduce the search space for the resolution of the design. The corresponding pedagogical positions relate to the application of knowledge drawn from across the curriculum and accessing knowledge at the 'point of need'. The second position, which is more commonly associated with technical matters, is much more comfortable if you need to write easily interpreted statements in a 'Programme of Study'. It leads to pedagogical positions associated with the need for sequenced learning prior to designing and hierarchies of concepts for which it is more straightforward to show progression. So it is not really surprising if challenges to the D&T curriculum lead to the emergence (re-emergence) of engineering systems terminology (structural, mechanical, electronic etc). These are of course concepts from the epistemology of engineering, where the essential language is mathematics, so there are inevitable tensions for those who hold to the first position concerning design epistemology. Aesthetic, economic, moral and technical values for designing (as they were once classified by the Assessment of Performance Unit for Design and Technology (APU) (Hicks et al, 1982:26), and hedonic values, which featured in the Annex to Tender invitation for the APU study (Roberts,1981) are not generally expressed mathematically And so whilst these two positions remain disconnected, one group or the other will inevitably feel outside of their comfort zone. It is a problem exacerbated by the longstanding difficulties that individual English people seem to have in embracing both Science and the Humanities.

The reality of course is that neither of these epistemological positions is accurate in relation to the nature of the problems that designers address. The epistemology of design is actually of a more fluid nature. Roman Architects knew the principles embedded in Vitruvius' *De Architectura* which covered both aesthetic and technical matters. They were used to construct many successful buildings, although they might not be quite the same and have been so rigorously tested as those available to modern architects. Vincenti (1990) has provided a fascinating account of design knowledge derived from a study of aeronautical history: *What Engineers Know and How They Know it*. Vincenti's categories of design knowledge are: fundamental design concepts; criteria and specifications; theoretical tools; quantitative data; practical considerations and design instrumentalities. The whole of this book is central to informing the current debates, but in relation to 'D&T' the final two in this list are the most significant. Consider these quotations:

> 5. Practical considerations. Theoretical tools and quantitative data are, by definition, precise and codifiable; they come mostly from deliberate research. They are not, however, by themselves sufficient. Designers also need for their work an array of less sharply defined considerations derived from experience in practice, considerations that frequently do not lend themselves to theorizing, tabulation, or programming into a computer. Such considerations are mostly learned on the job rather than in school or from books; they tend to be carried around, sometimes more or less unconsciously, in designers' minds. Frequently they are hard to find written down. The practice from which they derive necessarily includes not only design but production and operation as well, though such practice may not – typically is not – by the designers themselves.
> (Vincenti,1990: 217)

In relation to the APU's descriptions, Vincenti is referring to technical values.

> TECHNICAL values involve an appreciation and application of the following concepts: efficiency, and the ways in which input is compared with the resultant output; robustness; flexibility, and the ways in which the performance of a man-made object or system might be sensitive to change; precision, and the

qualities of fit and of fitness to purpose, valued either for their own sakes or as a means to an end; confidence, and the ways in which the possible reliability or unreliability of information is taken into account.   (Hicks et al, 1982: 26)

Regrettably, there seems to have been surprisingly little progress in defining this practical dimension of design epistemology since this APU study. Vincenti also moved deeper into this area through his consideration of design instrumentalites.

> 6. Design instrumentalities. Besides the analytical tools, quantitative data, and practical considerations required for their tasks, designers need to know how to carry out those tasks … the instrumentalities of the process – the procedures, ways of thinking, and judgmental skills by which it is done – nevertheless must be part of any anatomy of engineering knowledge. They give engineers the power, not only to effect designs where the form of the solution is clear at the outset, but also to seek solutions where some element of novelty is required.
> (op cit: 219)

[…and later in discussing these matters…]

> Finally, designers need the pragmatic judgmental skills required to seek out design solutions and make design decisions. Such skills like visual thinking, call for insight, imagination and intuition, as well as a feeling for elegance and aesthetics in technical design.   (ibid: 222)

From this brief overview, it is already evident that the two positions concerning design epistemology might turn out to be rather less distinct than their proponents would have you believe. Design problems are not really 'defined' or 'ill-defined' in some binary sense, but made up of a myriad of design problems, some more defined than others. Product design specifications (PDS) repeatedly demonstrate this. Design epistemology must embrace all aspects of the PDS, including the hedonistic concerns. That sounds quite dramatic when you write it, but consider the APU's description of hedonic values:

> HEDONIC values, which might involve an awareness of:
>
> 1. the role of vision. hearing, smell, taste and touch in attaching value phenomena through their direct appeal to the senses;
> 2. the role of appetite, desire, pleasure, pain, etc. in the evolution of products and systems;
> 3. the demands made on the configuration of man-made things and systems by the physiology and psychology of people;
> 4. the importance of hedonic factors in all forms of design activity and an ability to take them into account when designing or evaluating things in the man-made environment.   (Roberts, 1981)

To modernise this description 'man' would need to be deleted from 'man-made' which was an expression of its time, but surely these should be routine aspects of design epistemology by now. 'Design for function' and 'design for use' are now assumed to have been completed successfully in product design and manufacture (or customers would be entitled to refunds on products that were not fit for purpose). It is 'design for emotion' that distinguishes successful from unsuccessful products on the shelves of the 21st century. And in these terms, is it so hard to build bridges – to continue the engineering theme – between 'food' and some of the more technical design areas?

Design epistemology is clearly tricky, and it is no doubt a moving target, but there are some significant foundations already in place. Perhaps there are published reflections on Vitruvius' *De Architectura* from modern architects and Vincenti's *What Engineers Know and How They Know it: Analytical Studies from Aeronautical History* from modern aeronautical engineers. If not, developing an understanding of those elements that have stood the test of time and those that have evolved alongside the designing would be an excellent contribution to the literature. In the context of curriculum planning it is time that we had at least a temporary grip on design epistemology, because otherwise the debates become a hotbed of curriculum politics and design education is more important than that.

References

Hicks G (1982) *Understanding Design and Technology*, Assessment of Performance Unit

Roberts P H (1981) 'Annex to Tender invitation' *Understanding Design and Technology*, Assessment of Performance Unit

Vincenti W G (1990) *What Engineers Know and How They Know it: Analytical studies from aeronautical history*, The John Hopkins University Press, Baltimore and London

3. OTHERS' FIRST THOUGHTS ON DESIGN EPISTEMOLOGY

3.1 So what went wrong and why?
Stephanie Atkinson, Professor of Design and Technology Education, University of Sunderland

In *The Framework for the National Curriculum* written in 2011 the *Expert Panel* stated that along with Information and Communication Technology and Citizenship, Design and Technology (D&T) had weaker epistemological roots than other subjects that formed the National Curriculum (NC), and that as the NC needed to be slimmed down that these subjects should be removed and be reclassified as part of the Basic Curriculum (DfE 2011:24).

Their reasoning in the case of D&T was that the panel was not entirely persuaded by claims that D&T had what they termed "sufficient disciplinary coherence" (DfE 2011:24) to remain part of the NC. The Panel explained that their judgement was based on a view of disciplinary knowledge being "…a distinct way of investigating, knowing and making sense with a particular foci, procedures and theories" (DfE 2011:24).

Fortunately, after much lobbying from concerned D&T educationalists, researchers, industrialists and members of pertinent organizations and societies, the government chose not to accept the Expert Panel's view, and D&T remains as a subject in the NC. However, its position within schools remains precarious due to further government initiated educational changes, the causes of which, and the potential solutions to overcome these issues form the basis of this chapter.

In 1990 at the time of the introduction of the NC, D&T was placed in a strong curriculum position as the government made it mandatory for all pupils to study D&T up to the age of 16. However, in 2011 in a bid to raise standards by slimming down the number of subjects that pupils studied, the government decided that D&T would become an optional subject after Key Stage 3 meaning that fewer students would study it at Key Stage 4 and beyond. More recently in 2013 this decline was further exacerbated when D&T was not included in the new school performance measure, the English Baccalaureate (EBacc), where only English, Mathematics, History or Geography, the Sciences and a language are to be used when awarding an EBacc certificate. These two decisions have led many schools to cut down their D&T provision and in some secondary schools the subject has been removed completely from the curriculum.

So why has this lack of support for the subject come about, after what seemed a bright future as an essential part of every child's education in 1990? Returning to the view of the Expert Panel in 2011 in terms of there being a lack of coherence in D&T, I unfortunately have to admit to having some sympathy with this view. I am not referring to a lack of coherence in terms of what D&T sets out to achieve, as embodied in each iteration of D&T NC. I believe that each new version (1990; 1995; 2000; 2013) has provided a similar vision of the unique and essential contribution that the subject can offer as part of a broad balanced curriculum for all children. In 1990, the first document stated that:

> 'Design and Technology is about identifying needs, generating ideas, planning, making and testing to find best solutions. Pupils become aware of the ways in which technology is changing the home, workplace and lifestyles, and they will be better placed to respond to the employment needs of business and industry. They will learn that technological change cannot be reversed and will understand its enormous power and realise that its use has to be controlled. Technological capability will enable citizens to cope with a rapidly changing society, and meet the challenges of the 21st century.'

In 2013, the most recent document proclaimed that:

> 'Design and technology is an inspiring, rigorous and practical subject. Using creativity and imagination, pupils design and make products that solve real and relevant problems within a variety of contexts, considering their own and others' needs, wants and values. They acquire a broad range of subject knowledge and draw on disciplines such as mathematics, science, engineering, computing and art. Pupils learn how to take risks, becoming resourceful, innovative, enterprising and capable citizens. Through the evaluation of past and present design and technology, they develop a critical understanding of its impact on daily life and the wider world. High-quality design and technology education makes an essential contribution to the creativity, culture, wealth and well-being of the nation (DfE 2013).'

With each iteration, the stated aims have indicated a strong epistemological basis and something that those who have championed the subject over the years have supported and been inspired by.

However, what the Orders have tended not to do is prescribe exactly what is to be taught or how it is to be taught. This is understandable due to the very nature of the activities involved and the negative effect that such prescription would have on those activities. Nevertheless, back in 1990 Harrison aptly identified why this might be problematic for some teachers, when he stated:

> 'In order to ensure the delivery of a school subject of substance and real education value, the discipline of Design and Technology as a progressive learning experience for children must be explicit and in a form which may be consistently understood by the variety of teachers involved (Harrison 1990:87).'

Twenty-seven years later although there are many excellent examples of exciting, innovative D&T in schools across the country, we still have too many long serving and newly qualified teachers providing their pupils with D&T that falls short of meeting the subject's potential as a valuable and unique part of a child's education. It is also the case that many activities offered fail to persuade the general public, parents and even some pupils of the benefits that can be accrued from studying D&T. Such shortfalls support the Expert Panel's belief regarding the lack of coherence in the subject and also the inconsistency of understanding that Harrison indicated back in 1990. It is this perception of the subject by others that we as a D&T community have failed to successfully address over the years, even though many have tried.

An analysis of the available literature and my personal experience of being a teacher and active researcher of D&T for the past 50 years, indicate several factors that may have caused this situation to arise. Only two of these factors are targeted in this short chapter, as they appear to be central in determining how D&T was, and is taught, and in turn how it is perceived by the wider community, both of which link back to whether D&T has sufficient disciplinary coherence and sound epistemological roots.

Back in the late 1960s as a newly qualified teacher of Design, teaching Woodwork and Technical Drawing in a Leicestershire school I witnessed pockets of tangential development of the subject in certain Local Education Authorities such as Leicestershire, Nottingham and Bedford. These developments came out of what had been introduced into schools in the late 1880s as gender specific, craft-orientated subjects (Nicholl & Spendlove, 2016:126) where the predominant focus had been on the development of knowledge relating simply to the fabrication of artefacts (Dakers, 2006:2).

Throughout the 1970s and 1980s, the divisions between those who believed that the way forward for the subject was through a more technological systems and control approach that developed out of Project Technology; a vocational TVEI (Technical & Vocational Education Initiative) approach; a Design orientated approach, and even remaining as a craft based subject, became more and more marked. Interjections from protagonists of each approach were witnessed when vying for their ideas to be accepted as the chosen way forward for the subject. This was carried out in a manner that allowed those in positions of influence outside the D&T community to become aware of the divisions within the subject. In 1990 with the introduction of the first NC these divisions in direction did not disappear. The structure of the NC into separate areas, Resistant Materials; Electronics; Textile and Food encouraged the strands to develop independently rather than as a cohesive whole, thus continuing to indicate to those outside the D&T community that there was indeed a lack of coherence in the discipline. This perception of the subject has played a vital role in determining the position the subject finds itself in today.

It is only in the most recent NC document (DfE, 2013) that the segregation into separate strands has ceased to exist. The changes to the NC have also meant a re-design of the Key Stage 4 GCSE D&T examination so that it followed on from what is now being taught during Key Stages 1- 3.

The new single GCSE D&T examination should be a positive move with its greater concentration on building innovative iterative design processes through which students can explore, create and evaluate a range of outcomes across a breadth of contexts and materials (Edexcel, 2016) rather than continuing the split into five separate examinations. However, it does require secondary D&T teachers to have extensive breadth as well as depth of subject knowledge to meet the new requirements successfully and take the subject forward in the manner intended.

Teacher's subject knowledge, or lack of it, leads admirably into the second factor concerning the position of D&T today. It concerns the demise of in-depth initial teacher education for D&T teachers over recent years (e.g. Atkinson, 2009; 2012; Hardy, 2015). Instead of 4-year or 3-year undergraduate programmes teaching D&T subject knowledge and appropriate pedagogy over a sustained period of time, the majority of D&T teachers are now trained in one year as post-graduate students either in University or in work-based situations. So much educational pedagogy has to be packed into that year to meet Qualified Teacher Status Standards and Ofsted expectations that there is very limited time left for the development of a comprehensive understanding of the subject that is to be taught alongside how to convert that knowledge into an appropriate form for classroom situations (Atkinson, 2009). This is additionally exacerbated by the misalignment between subject knowledge gained on the many varied first degrees that applicants now study before deciding to become a D&T teacher. Gone are the days when students came into the teaching profession with D&T knowledge, skills and understanding to an appropriate depth. This is compounded further by the lack of uptake on continued professional development (CPD) courses offered by various providers, that would enable teachers to overcome their lack of subject knowledge once they were qualified and teaching in schools. Research data would suggest that this is due to limited school budgets with commitments other than CPD being prioritised, and a lack of time for busy teachers to devote to such activities, even if they are aware of their own needs. The spiral of pupils taught D&T poorly becoming the trainees without time or support to improve their subject knowledge, who then become the teachers of the next generation of pupils who in turn become the next generation of teachers and even the trainers of teachers is a spiralling picture that is all too evident (Atkinson, 2009, 2012) and one which plays into the hands of those outside the D&T community who see that there is a lack of "sufficient disciplinary coherence" in the subject.

This lack of belief in the benefits of the subject is particularly pertinent in terms of people responsible for educational changes that concern the place of D&T within the curriculum along with those who make decisions regarding the financial support required for training both new and existing teachers. We as a community must find a way to influence their perceptions of the subject. For no matter whether everyone within the D&T community believes in the subject's strong epistemological roots, disciplinary coherence and the subject's importance from a cultural, social and personal perspective (Barlex & Steeg, 2017), without the support of those who hold the purse strings and those who make national educational decisions, we will struggle to overcome the problems that have been highlighted in this chapter.

We are unable to alter what has happened in the past. However, we cannot afford to be complacent about the future. If D&T is to survive we as a community must overcome the internal differences that do still exist, and only then will we be seen by others to be united in our beliefs. When we can display a robust disciplinary coherence that clearly supports the strong epistemological roots that we know the subject has, then we may once again receive the external support that our subject deserves and requires to maintain its important role in the education of future generations.

References

Atkinson S (2009) 'Are Design and Technology teachers able to meet the challenges inherent in the theme for this conference 'D&T – A Platform for Success'?'. In E Norman (Ed.) *Design and Technology Education: an International Journal*, 14 (3), 8-20

Atkinson S (2012) 'What Constitutes good learning in Technology Education: How can we ensure that technology education graduates can provide it? *TERC*, Griffith University, December 2012, 1-13

Barlex D & Steeg T (2017). *Re-Building Design & Technology In the Secondary School Curriculum: Version 2*. Accessed from https://dandtfordandt.wordpress.com 1.05.17

Department for Education (2011) *The Framework for the National Curriculum. A report by the Expert Panel for the National Curriculum review*, Department for Education, London

Department for Education, (2013) *National Curriculum in England: design and technology programmes of study*, Department for Education, London

Dakers J (2006) 'Introduction'. In J. Dakers (Ed.) *Defining Technological Literacy: Towards an epistemological framework*, Palgrave Macmillan, Houndmills Bassingstoke

Edexcel, *GCSE (9-1) Design and Technology*, (2016), London: Pearson Education Ltd

Hardy A L (2015) *Why has the number of teenagers taking design and technology GCSE dropped?* [online]. The Conversation. Available at: https://theconversation.com/why-has-the-number-of-teenagers-taking-design-and-technology-gcse-dropped-46361 [Accessed 06.04.17]

Harrison G B (1990). 'Frameworks for Curriculum Development in Design and Technology'. In J S Smith (Ed) *3rd National Conference Design and Technology Educational Research & Curriculum Development*, Loughborough: Loughborough University, 87-95

Nicholl B & Spendlove D (2016) 'Academic Tasks in Design and Technology Education'. In M. de Vries, S. Fletcher, S. Kruse, P. Labudde, M. Lang, I. Mammes, C. Max, D. Münk, B. Nichol, J.Strobel and M. Winterbottom (Eds.) *Technology Education Today: International Perspectives,* Waxmann, Münster, 125 -146

3.2 How did the expert panel conclude that D&T should be moved to a basic curriculum?

Alison Hardy, Senior Lecturer, Nottingham Institute of Education, Nottingham Trent University

The dramatic decline of D&T as a core component of the English National Curriculum is well documented with some reasons for the decline suggested, including its non-inclusion from school performance measures and its disapplication as a compulsory qualification for all 16 year olds (Bell et al., 2017; Design and Technology Association, 2015; Hardy, 2015). Yet it was the Expert Panel's (Department for Education, 2011) report that focussed the D&T community's mind on the subject's epistemology and knowledge-base, matters that have often not been at the forefront of either D&T research or debate. The report asserted that D&T had insufficient disciplinary coherence to warrant its continued inclusion in the National Curriculum. Rather than discussing whether D&T has disciplinary coherence or not, or whether it should be part of a core or basic curriculum, this chapter explores why the Panel may have come to that conclusion. It begins with the report's political origins and the prevailing ideology of the purpose of education. Once this is understood it becomes easier to understand the Panel's opinion, which is born out from interviews with D&T teachers about D&T's contribution to a general education. Finally, a way forward is suggested.

The Expert Panel report was commissioned early in 2011 by Michael Gove, the then Secretary of State for Education and a Conservative MP in the Coalition government. Conservatives have long extolled the centrality of knowledge to education and equality (see Lord Baker's comments in the 2010 House of Commons report). And when, after the 2010 general election, Michael Gove became Secretary of State and Nick Gibb Schools Minister there was an opportunity to 'slim down' the National Curriculum to one that taught young people the 'best that has been said and thought' (Gibbs, 2016). It needs to be recognized where Gove and Gibb were gaining their ideas from. Gibb and Gove had publicly lauded the work of Hirsch (2006) and Willingham (2009)who focus on the value of learning knowledge and facts, specifically 'general, all-purpose knowledge' (Hirsch 2006:12), knowledge that forms part of a general education (Willingham 2009). In drawing on Hirsch and Willingham they had found 'evidence' to support their views:

> 'The work of cognitive scientists, most helpfully analysed by the University of Virginia's Daniel T Willingham and buttressed by the research of educationists like E D Hirsch, has shown that the best way to develop critical thinking skills is to ensure all children have a firm grounding in a traditional knowledge-based curriculum.' (Department for Education and Gove, 2014)

By placing thinking skills as a subordinate of knowledge, Gove and Gibb shifted away from the 2007 National Curriculum that some thought had emphasized skills to the detriment of knowledge. Consequently, the Panel was commissioned to:

> 'Develop a National Curriculum that provides young people with the knowledge they need to move confidently and successfully through their education.'

Underpinned by a belief that the National Curriculum should 'ensure that all children have the opportunity to acquire a core of essential knowledge in the key subject disciplines'. In the Expert Panel report, knowledge is defined as 'subject knowledge' that constitutes the concepts, facts, processes, language, narratives and conventions, and is regarded as 'powerful'. Here the report references Young (2008) as its source for 'powerful'. Therefore, to understand the Expert Panel's stance on knowledge, it is necessary to understand Young's 'powerful knowledge'.

Professor Michael Young has written extensively on knowledge and social justice through education. His opinion is that the purpose of schooling is to 'enable young people to acquire the knowledge that for most of them cannot be acquired at home or in the community' (Young, 2011:150); he defines this knowledge as theoretical not everyday knowledge, and specialised in how it is produced and transmitted (Young, 2013). He argues that powerful knowledge originates in specialist institutions (e.g. universities), which is transmitted in other specialist institutions (i.e. schools). His argument for the importance of powerful knowledge is underpinned by the principle of social justice and entitlement - for young people to gain access to universities they need to learn the powerful knowledge that originates there, which can only be done in schools (Young and Muller, 2013). Furthermore, powerful knowledge 'is embodied in different domains' (Young, 2011:151), and therefore is discipline-based (Young and Muller, 2013). Strong, disciplinary coherent school subjects have a clear form of knowledge, which originates in universities and research centres. Disciplinary coherence is a subject that has a strongly defined boundary between itself and other subjects (Bernstein, 2000).

Therefore, it could be concluded the Expert Panel decided a coherent National Curriculum should only consist of subjects that teach 'powerful knowledge' whose knowledge originates in universities and research institutions. And it is at this point the argument for including D&T in the National Curriculum unravels. As an educational construct (Bell, et al., 2017), D&T's knowledge is not derived from a single discipline; instead it draws on several disciplines, such as art, anthropology, and physics. Unfortunately, this perception of D&T's incoherence as a discipline is corroborated by my research (for example Hardy 2016).

In 2014, I interviewed D&T teachers and students from two schools, and asked for their perception of the contribution D&T made to an individual's education. Their responses were grouped into three themes:

1. Responses relating to the uniqueness of D&T, which could suggest some coherence about the subject which makes it distinct from other subjects;

2. Responses about competency or skills that are not limited by specialist knowledge curriculum;

3. Responses that relate to other subjects and their content, which would indicate a disciplinary incoherence as the participants would be suggesting that D&T exists because of other subjects.

In the first theme, the predominant view was that children were taught to critique products and their impact on the environment. A lesser view was that D&T's unique contribution was to teach vocational skills, an argument which disqualifies it as an essential subject in the National Curriculum taught to all children. If the perception is that D&T is a subject which prepares children for D&T related professions then all children do not need access to it – only those who have an aptitude or inclination to progress into a D&T-related career. The value of learning how to design and make products was rarely mentioned. In the second theme, participants talked about individuals learning skills to look after themselves that meant they could do DIY, cook and sew; skills that rely on everyday knowledge and do not necessarily require a specialist institution. Other responses mentioned learning generic, transferrable skills such as team working, and problem-solving. Neither learning generic skills or 'domestic' skills are forms of knowledge deemed essential to the National Curriculum by the Expert Panel. The fewest responses were grouped into the final theme; here the teachers and students mentioned learning about materials, using maths and drawing, which would 'help them in art'. This analysis suggests these teachers and students held a narrow perspective of D&T's knowledge, and instead emphasized how students learnt to become competent in skills useful for domestic life and future employment.

Although a small study it does have implications for D&T, how it is understood by those within its community and how it is understood by outsiders. It would be interesting to conduct further research asking D&T teachers what discipline they see as the origins of D&T's knowledge, to determine their understanding of D&T's specialist knowledge. I would suspect many would find it a challenging question, and others would dispute its value as a research question. However, as the current education ideology emphasizes the importance of knowledge it is timely to encourage the D&T community to engage in answering the questions - What powerful knowledge is taught in D&T? And from where does it originate?

References

Bell D, Wooff D, McLain M and Morrison-Love D, (2017) 'Analysing design and technology as an educational construct: an investigation into its curriculum position and pedagogical identity', *The Curriculum Journal,* , 1-20

Bernstein B (2000) *Pedagogy, Symbolic Control and Identity: Theory, research, critique.* Revised Edition, Rowman and Littlefield, Lanham, Maryland

Department for Education (2011) *The Framework for the National Curriculum. A report by the Expert Panel for the National Curriculum review,* Department for Education, London

Department for Education and Gove M (2014) *Michael Gove speaks about the future of education reform (Speech given to Education reform Summit 10/7/2014)* [online]. Department for Education. Available at: https://www.gov.uk/government/speeches/michael-gove-speaks-about-the-future-of-education-reform [Accessed 03/04 2017]

Design and Technology Association (2015) *Designed and Made in Britain...?* [online]. DATA. Available at: http://bit.ly/1n1vm9J [Accessed 01/14 2016]

Gibbs N (2016) *What is a Good Education in the 21st Century?,* Hild Bede College, Durham University, Department for Education

Hardy A L (2015) *Why has the number of teenagers taking design and technology GCSE dropped?* [online]. The Conversation. Available at: https://theconversation.com/why-has-the-number-of-teenagers-taking-design-and-technology-gcse-dropped-46361 [Accessed 07/22 2016]

Hardy A L (2016) An assortment box of views: different perceptions of D&T's purpose and structure. In: *PATT2016 - Technology Education for 21st Century Skills Conference, Utrecht, 23-26 August.* Utrecht, Netherlands

Hirsch E D (2006) *The Knowledge Deficit: Closing the shocking education gap for American children,* Houghton Mifflin Company, Boston

Willingham D T (2009) *Why Don't Students Like School?: A cognitive scientist answers questions about how the mind works and what it means for the classroom,* John Wiley & Sons

Young M F D (2013) 'Overcoming the crisis in curriculum theory: a knowledge-based approach', *Journal of Curriculum Studies,* 45 (2), 101-118.

Young M F D (2011) 'What are schools for?', *Educação, Sociedade & Culturas,* 32

Young M F D (2008) *Bringing Knowledge Back In: From social constructivism to social realism in the sociology of education,* Routledge, Abingdon

Young M F D and Muller J (2013) 'On the powers of powerful knowledge', *Review of Education,* 1 (3), 229-250

3.3 Some thoughts on locating design knowledge
Steve Keirl, Reader in Design Education, Goldsmiths, University of London

The context
These 'first thoughts' on design epistemology are contextualised against six premises. First, for democracy to survive, education (which is not training) is a necessary and common good. Second, these thoughts address 'general education', that is, education that is given to every child on a continuous basis over their compulsory years of schooling. Third, we cannot in any way define what it is that makes us human without acknowledging our intimate relationship with technologies. Fourth, for the purposes of this exercise, 'technologies' are seen as *anything the species has created or made*. This encompassing understanding would include laws, political systems, education, the arts, languages, offspring, food, and so on. Thus, fifth, all technologies are the result of designerly acts. Sixth, there is a vast void between the education currently on offer (almost anywhere in the world) and the deep significance to our existences of designed technologies.

Design matters. Design is an essence of the being of every person; it is at the core of why humanity is where it is today; and, it is key to our personal and collective futures. Design and design education are clearly important but how can design knowledge be understood?

(Re-)positioning knowledge, (re-)designing curriculum in which direction?
Education is about learning but, as we know, learning takes multiple forms. One crude and currently dominant notion of education depends on the idea that 'knowledge' is something detached, objective, out-there, and identifiable. I say 'crude' and 'depends' because such constructions not only belittle the idea of knowledge itself but also, in sinister ways, are used (by elites and policy-makers) to dictate what must be learned. In turn, for reasons of control of both curriculum and its stakeholders, such packaged knowledge must be readily measurable and testable. It is no surprise that the capitalist club of 34 elite countries – the Organisation for Economic Cooperation and Development (OECD) – has driven a decades-long agenda to establish testing regimes in national language, mathematics and science which set pupil against pupil, school against school, and country against country in league tables. In the early 1970s, authors such as Ivan Illich were warning of the dangers of 'institutionalizing' knowledge (Illich, 1973).
When working on the question of design epistemology we ignore this scenario at our peril. The reinforcement of a restricted, subject-based curriculum (subjects being prescribed knowledge packages) has intentionally created a commodification of pupils, schools and states with the principal goal of serving 'the market' (capitalism). Why else would such an organization be the driver of such an agenda?

Imagine now a curriculum of different 'subjects' – ones not framed by knowledge packages. I would nominate (for example) ethics, philosophy, drama, design, sustainability, futures. What would count as knowledge here? Our first step might be to get away from mis-applying Ryle's (1949) distinction of *propositional* and *procedural* knowledge – often described as 'knowing that…' and 'know-how' and often misunderstood as being mutually exclusive. Deeper study of (Design and) Technology (D&T) education shows us that it is fraught with multiple binaries that are not cases of *either-or* but, rather, are cases of *at-once-both*. (Keirl, 2015) So debates about whether D&T is academic or practical, specialist or general, a subject or a field, are spurious in trying to locate its identity.

The historical baggage of many current Western models of education traces back to The Academy wherein lie *disciplines*, each defined by an identifiable and distinct *body of knowledge*. It is on these that school subjects have been founded and the tighter the package of knowledge, the more 'academic' the subject has been deemed. Against such an historical pedigree and the OECD agenda, what chance would something as encompassing as Design and Technology have? Might the curriculum game be looked at differently? The answer to this comes, first, from foregrounding some of the attributes of design (as noun, verb or adjective) and, second, from seeing knowledge in different ways.

Seeing design ...
Design is a powerful word in the English language. It has noun-value and can perform equally well as subject and object – whether grammatically, practically or philosophically so. It has verb-value and can signal action, intention and creation. It has adjective-value and can clarify, enhance or specify meaning. Thus the grammars of design as a holistic enterprise emerge. Within the field, design has a richness of concepts and practices that can collectively be called design discourses. It also has its sub-fields - just as do the arts, mathematics, languages, and science.

Design has special temporal relations. To design is to change one set of circumstances into another from one point in time to another. Because design is intentional it is orientated toward the future. Design is an expression of the will and resists determinism. Design *is* change. Design is provisional, at once locating and dislocating.

The act of designing blends a spectrum of mental dispositions: of imagination, critique, reason, creativity, reflection, incubation, analysis, synthesis, determination, and more etc. Design is unsettled, unsettling, messy, gregarious, opportunistic, playful, confrontational and satisfying.

Designing demands the weighing of competing variables and the sensitive engagement of rich assemblages of values yet, once the design is 'out there' it becomes the focus of varied usage and critique. Previously unattributed values are attributed to the design and it becomes part of the existential background (Gadamer, 1977) of its user/s, location/s or culture/s. Thus, design is aconsequential, that is, despite the intentions of the designer/s, the nature of the design's consequences is never certain (Tenner, 1997; Ihde, 2006).

Design knowledge resembles theoretical knowledge in that it is ever provisional, tentative, and open to critique, moderation and refinement. Design knowledge is possible knowledge, knowledge-in-the-making and, thus, *design is meaning in the making*. As with research outcomes, any design is itself a (hopefully) modest contribution to new knowledge. This is certainly the case for any committed designer-at-work but the design outcomes are also a potential contribution to that which can be *known* in the world at large.

As with any field of human endeavour that is the subject of theorization, creativity, research and production, design enjoys its ongoing debates, theoretical disputes, attempts at taxonomy, paradigm shifts, and emergent positions. Witness, for example, articulated cases for sets of *design principles* (see e.g. Mayall, 1979; McDonough, 1998) or sample a host of design manifestos (backspace.com, 2009/2014)

As a provisional summary at this point, we might tentatively suggest that design knowledge is *knowing all of the above as a rich collection of design conditions capable of richly informing design practices*. The processes involved both in learning these conditions and in practising these practices over many years position design as triple meaning-maker: for the designer through design activity; for the user-critic through the use-critique of the design outcome/s; and for the community at large through the resultant dialogues.

Seeing knowledge differently...

If we now turn back to epistemology and the ways in which knowledge can be understood we can move on from the orthodoxies of the Academy, disciplines, subjects and prescriptions of knowledge. Such positivist mechanics, despite still being the stuff of many school systems, have been strongly critiqued for over a hundred years. To locate design knowledge or, perhaps better, an epistemology of design, I would suggest we must first draw on critiques of epistemological orthodoxy – critiques which seek to displace analytical-positivist thinking to make way for more inclusive alternatives.

Design knowledge certainly engages with empiricism in that sense-data inform both mental or physical design activity. Tacit knowledge is drawn upon as are intuition and abstract thinking. When design knowledge grows by iterative processes, constructivist epistemology is foregrounded. In design engagements, distinctions between subject-object and analysis-synthesis blur. In turn, major theoretical schools have informed epistemological critiques. For example, postmodernism (viz: the pluralized *knowledges*) and feminist theory (on power distribution) have opened up new ways of seeing and engaging in the world.

Both of these fields have been influenced by critical theory which problematizes theory of any kind as being context-bound by history, culture and subjectivity. As Buchanan says: 'Critical theory…is a highly reflexive enterprise…never satisfied with asking what something means or how it works, it also has to ask what is at stake in asking such questions in the first place.' (Buchanan, 2010:100). In this theoretical field, 'critical' is used as an opposite to 'analytical'. Basically, things cannot be, and ought not to be, taken for granted.

Critical theorist Jurgen Habermas (1971; 1984; 1987), in developing his *theory of communicative action* (an apt tag for design perhaps) highlights the importance of understanding knowledge as something much more than just out-there, identifiable, and mind-independent and argues that there are differing *human interests* at play in what constitutes knowledge and in how or why we might want that knowledge. His work points to how governmental and educational systems actually work to exclude some sections of society from full knowledge (and learning).

We can bring Habermas's work readily to Design and Technology education and, more particularly, to design epistemology, by considering a basic illustration of the three knowledge interests. Humans have a *technical knowledge interest* which amounts to a rather uncritical can-do. It is about utility and function. Then there is the *practical-hermeneutic knowledge interest* where knowledge and learning are applied as action-on-the-world and meaning-making emerges – hermeutics being the theory and methodology of *interpretation*. Ultimately, there is the *critical-emancipatory knowledge interest* whereby we are capable of critiquing the very knowledge and learning *itself* in order to have rich, well-informed, critical decision-making capacities. Here matters of spirituality, ontology and fulfilment meet to position individuals as independent, emancipated (i.e. not bound by any particular orthodoxy) beings-in-the-world.

I would argue that design epistemology (as well as any epistemology of technology) must attend not only to identifying that which is special about design knowledge or technological knowledge but it must also uphold a continuously foregrounded critique across the three knowledge interests. To do so would maintain healthy distance from the many pitfalls that come with orthodox positions on knowledge. It would also serve to inform, celebrate and articulate any emergent position on design epistemology or, indeed, a fluidity of design epistemology. In turn, school curricula and educational policymakers may begin to understand the educational power and the social good that is design education.

Quality design education needs robust design epistemology.
If D&T education is seen as simply designing and making stuff then we might as well go home. The game has to be lifted – within as well as beyond the profession. If learning and knowledge result in meaning-making then design learning and knowledge result in a particularly powerful form of meaning-making (so long as all three human knowledge interests are pursued).

One of design's epistemological problems lies in how it sees itself in the discipline game. I say 'game' because of the traditional orthodoxies that would talk of disciplinary knowledge in the prescriptive packaged sense of there being 'branches' of knowledge. I would argue that design *is* a discipline but I would also be cautious in how I engage with questions of its particular knowledge and becoming ensnared in the language games of stilted (rather than enlightened) curriculum debate. We can also consider design as: inter-disciplinary (operating between disciplines); cross-disciplinary (bridging disciplines); multi-disciplinary (engaging many disciplines); but, we should also consider it (after my colleagues at Goldsmiths) as anti-disciplinary (working against disciplines).

We should also consider the potent political and curricular forces at work that would marginalize and/or erode design as the powerful educational tool that it is. The STEM agenda with its simple populism with teachers and politicians alike is a ready example of a curriculum push that renders rich design education invisible. So-called computer 'science' and vocational education have the same effect. From a *human knowledge interest* perspective, all such examples remain largely in the technical realm.

I believe that design epistemology could do well to draw itself more fully into two phenomena – *the existential* and *democracy*. Design works in, through and for both. Design must respect our four realms of co-existence – human beings with each other, with the planet, with other species and with technologies (Keirl, 2010). Equally, design must work for democracy by being democratic in its practices, by being part of democratic schooling and by advancing democracy itself (Keirl, 2001; Baynes, 2005; Keirl, 2006). Design activism is a valid enterprise of citizenship while design apathy is a blight on society. There are good personal, cultural, social and political reasons for a rich design education that celebrates rich design knowledges. Fulfilment, creativity, imagination and empathy are all social goods that design can nurture.

Education is an ultimate public good, vital to all people (our co/existences) and to how we organise our societies (democracy). Design education has a key role to play in such a good. Design epistemology is about neither privileging knowledge nor privileged knowledge and when design epistemology fulfils all three knowledge interests it will be at its richest and most powerful as a field of learning and meaning-making for all.

References

Backspace.com, (2009/2014), *100+ years of Design Manifestos*
URL: http://backspace.com/notes/2009/07/design-manifestos.php

Baynes K (2005), *Design and Democracy: Speculations on the radical potential of design, design practice and design education*, The Design and Technology Association, Wellesbourne, UK

Buchanan I (2010) *A Dictionary of Critical Theory*, Oxford University Press, Oxford

Gadamer H-G (1977) *Philosophical Hermeneutics*, (Trans. Linge, D.E.), University of California Press, Berkeley

Habermas J (1971) *Knowledge and Human Interests*, Beacon, Boston

Habermas J (1984) *The Theory of Communicative Action Volume One: Reason and the rationalization of society*, Beacon, Boston

Habermas J (1987) *The Theory of Communicative Action Volume Two: Lifeworld and system – a critique of functionalist reason*, Beacon, Boston

Ihde D (2006) 'The Designer Fallacy and Technological Imagination'. In J R Dakers (2006) (Ed.), *Defining Technological Literacy: Towards an epistemological framework*, Palgrave Macmillan, Basingstoke, 121-131

Illich I (1973) *Tools for Conviviality*, Harper & Row, New York

Keirl S (2001) 'As if Democracy Mattered… design, technology and citizenship or 'Living with the temperamental elephant''. In E W L Norman & P H Roberts (Eds.), *Design and Technology Educational Research and Curriculum Development: The emerging international research agenda*, Loughborough University, Loughborough, U.K.

Keirl S (2006) 'Ethical technological literacy as democratic curriculum keystone'. In J R Dakers (Ed.) (2006), *Defining Technological Literacy: Towards an epistemological framework*, Palgrave Macmillan, Basingstoke, 81-102

Keirl S (2010) 'Critiquing and Designing as Thinking Tools for Technology Education for Sustainable Co-existence'. In R Hansen & S Petrina (Eds.), *Proceedings of the Technological Learning and Thinking: Culture, Design, Sustainability, Human Ingenuity Conference*, Vancouver, BC, 17-19 June, 2010, 531-540
URL: http://m1.cust.educ.ubc.ca/conference/index.php/TLT/2010/paper/view/57/5

Keirl S (2015) "Seeing' and 'interpreting' the Human-Technology phenomenon'. In P J Williams, A Jones & C Buntting (Eds.), *The Future of Technology Education*, Springer, Dordrecht, 13-34

Mayall W H (1979), *Principles in Design*, Design Council, London

McDonough W 'The Hannover Principles: Design for sustainability', (McDonough & Partners, Charlottesville, VA) in P Ellyard (1998) *Ideas for the New Millenium*, Melbourne University Press, Melbourne

Ryle G (1949), *The Concept of Mind*, Hutchinson, London

Tenner E (1997), *Why Things Bite Back: Technology and the revenge of unintended consequences,* Vintage, New York

3.4 How we know, what we should know: The building blocks of cultural awareness in design education
Graham Newman, School of Communication, Royal College of Art

I know what I know as a designer. I know how to explain what I know to other designers. Explaining how I know what I know to a non-design audience is harder to explain.

So what exactly is it that designers know? This question gives me an opportunity to reflect on my own career as a designer, educator and now, a design researcher. It's an important question to ask and discuss with practitioners as it raises questions about design within the current educational debate, and how might we improve on nurturing our incubated future designers in higher education.

This article is framed around a discussion on design epistemology with the graphic designer David Hitner, co-founder of Studio Small. David is a designer who can explain what he does, and what he knows, very well to a non-design audience; his clients. This goes some way to explaining why he and Guy Marshall run one of the best graphic design studios in the world. Broadly speaking David warranted my claims of a necessity for students and design educators, certainly those of us in communication design, to hardwire what I believe remain the fundamental building blocks of design epistemology: rules, critical reflection, collaboration and research.

In addition, I believe that as much as we can claim current undergraduate design education gives students a reasonable grounding in the fundamentals of their intended career, it is as imperative that they understand "why" they are doing something as much as "what" they are doing. The story of the work is as important as the final execution. They are one and the same.

Understand the rules, then break them
This sits within the atelier tradition of learning from a master craftsman. Much as we rightly allow students to naturally develop their lines of conceptual enquiry, it is imperative that they understand the fundamentals of what good design is. Furthermore, as the majority of design educators are also in professional practice; it is their responsibility to give all their expertise away. Quoting Paul Arden: "Give away everything you know, and more will come back".

I maintain the canon of modernist design rules, forged at the Bauhaus and Ulm should be compulsory learning for students to understand why a design solution works. And then understand how to reverse engineer these principles to breaking point.

DH: Ravensbourne College had a very strong typographic bias, it was more applied than some other design courses. You learnt a lot about rules, how things work, why they work, and what doesn't work. I've always argued that it's important to know the rules in order to start to break them or adapt them.

Upon leaving the LCP in 1991 I went to work for Factory Records and the Haçienda nightclub as a junior designer under the creative direction of John Macklin. John came from an engineering background and was a graduate of UMIST. I received a design education from LCP, and a design training from John. Our starting point on all Factory projects was a rigorous literature review of the history of graphic design and how might we interpret and develop our ideas based on these principles. What was the big idea and the rationale? This scaffolding allowed us to experiment with technology and printing processes. We never followed trend or set out to design for anyone other than ourselves; looking back I am still very proud of the work we produced together.

Question, research, edit, prototype
DH: Editing is really important in design, and the best designers are the ones that can edit their own work. Filtering ideas, knowing how to edit your own work, knowing what's of use, and what isn't; what you can and can't build your design concepts around. You also need to deep dive the rich history of design and certain designers to underpin your work.

At Factory, John was rigorous in framing design solutions within the context of graphic design history, and ruthless in getting what he wanted out of me, the brief and the budget. We agonized over colour, typeface, paper stock and printing techniques for the Hacienda's flyers, which usually only had a shelf life of 2 weeks. I produced blizzards of layout paper sketches whilst reviewing the literature of Emil Ruder, Armin Hoffman, Herb Lubalin et al. Most of my work got trashed. Then we went to the pub to discuss typography. In hindsight, having 2 full time designers on a record company/nightclub payroll now seems very exuberant. Perhaps it was at the time. That was how Factory and the Haçienda worked, and as such both businesses went bust very shortly after we left.

Empathise and collaborate
This is not just teamwork, it's engagement within design institutions, across schools. I believe this is the weakest part of the current design school framework and this is a plea for more collaborative, cross disciplinary project activity.

Tony Wilson, Factory's Generalissimo, always supported our design decisions, given he probably didn't know what the eventual outcomes were, but that was always the way he had worked with Peter Saville. Wilson was convinced that great music, art and culture is derived from the notion of praxis: "You learn why you do something by actually doing it". Factory was successful in shaping youth and popular culture because of Wilson's vision of multidisciplinary cross-collaboration. He always went on record during interviews stating "The Factory story is not about me, it's about the 150 people I have around me".

I have attempted, with varying degrees of success, to replicate this embracement of collaboration in my own career; having been fortunate enough to being involved with graphic design, pop videos, sound recording, photo shoots and currently, working in collaboration with the RCA's Visual Communications students as well as my own MRes researchers on the future of the book and the library (the RCAs Book Test Unit).

> DH: Most of our projects have an element of collaboration with other creatives whether it be a photographer or a product designer, so this is very important. At Ravensbourne we did a few projects with the product and fashion students. I think that really helped me. If you are on a design communications course, you are solely focused on design communications, but when you enter work you never work in a bubble. Creatively, it helps to collaborate as well. Pooling these collaborative skills together delivers a much stronger solution for our clients.

Collaborating across disciplines in design schools not only encourages students to think outside of their own practice, but gives them an understanding that there are other stakeholders in a project's success. Understanding and empathizing with someone else's point of view as a student is a valuable, transportable skill that I don't see enough of. It may get you hired and make you more money as well.

Above all, tell the story
I believe we need to encourage young people to have a broader, rather than deeper understanding of the design narrative. We tell stories with words (Twitter) and pictures (Instagram) now more than ever, and this trend will inevitably continue using smart technology.

> DH: We believe now that you can't separate the word from the pictures. It's as important what a design says as what it looks like. This is something we weren't taught in design education. What a design says is as important as what it looks like. I think students are very much pushed towards the style, the visual. Actually the words are as important, particularly when you are working across physical and digital media.

Being able to write about design in a way that's vaguely comprehensible is one of the hardest things I have undertaken in my career. Putting ideas into words – telling the story – involves the same rigor and pain as turning vaporous ideas into design substance. I sincerely would like to see more communication design courses include critical reading and writing as part of an undergraduate's education. The discipline of writing is as important as the discipline of design itself and I firmly believe these two now co-exist, as do the design practitioner and the design researcher.

Briefly returning to Wilson, who incidentally trained as a journalist, he often said to me: "If it's a choice between the truth and the myth, print the myth."

Conclusion

Above all else, what I know and how I know it, and I suspect the vast majority of designers in practice and education would agree with me, is based on simply getting out there and immersing oneself into the rich history of design. I suspect the "millennials" do not do enough of this. A survey published by Adobe Education last year identified creativity and technology as key generation differentiators for young people in the UK. For design students, these differentiators need to be substantiated with what has been discussed earlier. We can cluster these design building blocks as "cultural awareness".

As designers we need to be very culturally aware. And that doesn't just mean learning about other designers; it's about learning about design in the more broader context. The more culturally aware, the more reference points there are to pull on. I think ultimately this is a gut feeling. You do what you do based on your experience and knowledge. You have to make the decision that you feel what is right. It is subjective based on your knowledge. As the saying goes, if you want to understand the animals, get out into the jungle.

Acknowledgement

The author is indebted to David Hitner who generously provided time to discuss his work throughout this article.

3.5 Knowledge by design
Tristram Shepard, Freelance Design Education Consultant and Publisher

I want to explore the particular body of knowledge that belongs to design education and which is concerned with design methodology. Designers are highly knowledgeable of the various problem-solving techniques involved, the advantages and disadvantages of each and when it is most appropriate to use them. Knowledge of a specific material or production technology is usually only acquired as and when needed to meet the requirements of a proposed solution to a problem.

Design education is currently located, and somewhat severely constrained, more or less exclusively in the curriculum subject of Design and Technology. The new Awarding Organization D&T specifications contain extensive and explicit coverage of a knowledge of the properties, processes and tools relating to traditional materials, while only superficially mentioning design skills and learning about people's physical and psychological needs and the interface between users and products, places and communications.

While I have no wish to see a knowledge of design methodologies examined through a 'written paper' or subject to a series of atomistic coursework 'tick-boxes', if they were presented in more detail and with greater clarity in curriculum and examination requirements they might come to be more widely and effectively taught and used in on-going project work.

Iterative design
Ever since I first engaged with Design Education in schools back in the mid 1970s there has been frequent debate about what the 'design' in design education actually refers to. Personally I find no need for a rigid, finite definition and can accept that it is an amorphous concept that changes according to context and circumstances. The other major discussion topic has of course been about the so-called and much misunderstood 'Design Process' which over time has evolved from being a straight line to a concertina of convergent and divergent thinking, to a circular shape and a zig-zag. My own version of the process is perhaps more of a Jackson Pollock affair with a series of design skills applied in spontaneous, random, multi-layered actions that somehow form fascinating rhythmic and unique patterns that are subtly different in each design task, with the different colours representing the various design skills of identifying and investigating problems, generating and developing ideas, planning and organization, evaluation and communication. However a more structured representation (Fig 3.1) illustrates their interdependence more clearly And these skills are inextricably linked: one can't be done without at least one other.

> In design education students need to acquire the knowledge that:
> - designing is not a fixed, step-by-step process;
> - designing involves a rich mixture of different methods, carefully chosen and applied as and when appropriate;

- *the main design skills are identifying and investigating problems, generating and developing ideas, planning and organization, communication and evaluation;*
- *successful design is rarely easy or straightforward and often only emerges over a period of time after a creatively messy but enjoyable struggle.*

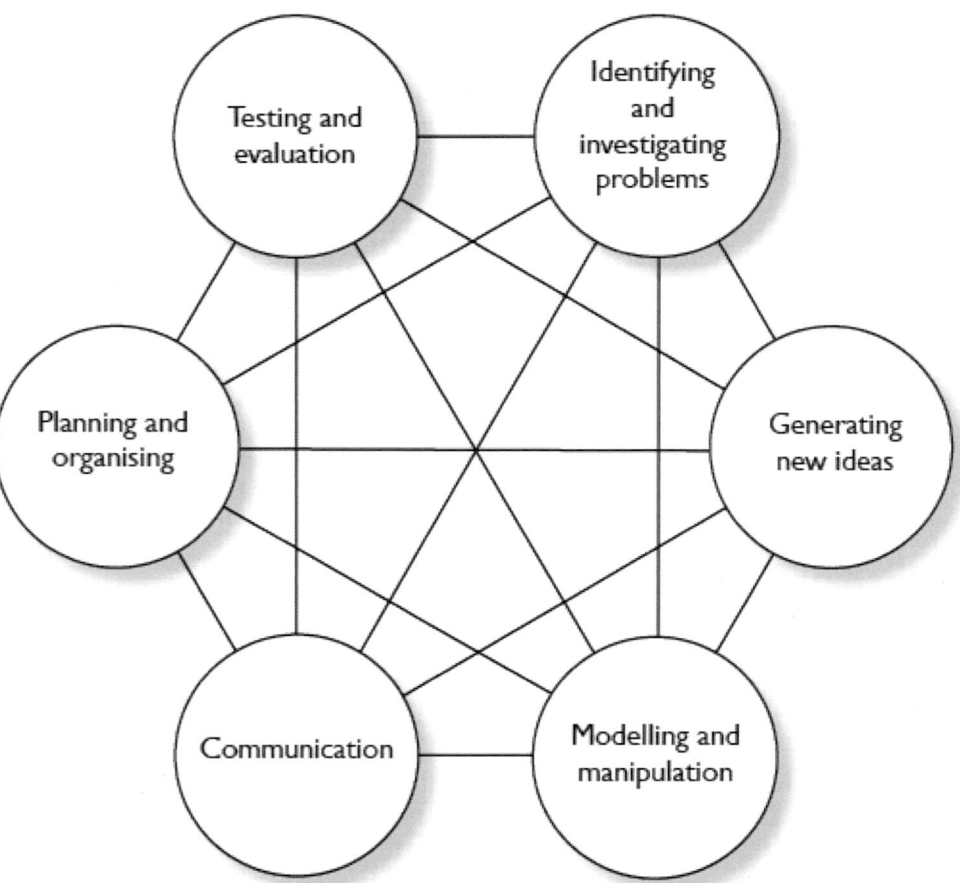

Figure 3.1 Structured representation of designing

Identifying opportunities for design

Most commercial design work tends to originate from a brief supplied by a client. The target market is usually clearly defined and the solution must fit within the brand guidelines. Although the client might appear to know what they require, the designer is sometimes able to come up with proposals that present ideas that the client 'didn't know they even wanted'. Many commissions emerge out of much broader organizational marketing strategies where the availability and promotion of the product, place or communication is as important as the design itself. In this context the traditional disciplines of design, such as product, graphics, textiles, spatial, etc., are increasingly disappearing and are being replaced by broader multi-disciplinary teams specializing in, for example, Service Design, Design Thinking, User Experience Design, Interaction Design and Information Architecture.

There are however, other designers and design companies that work the other way round - identifying potential new products that they then pitch to investors: this is the most demanding and risky, but perhaps more rewarding, way of working.

> *In design education students need to acquire the knowledge that:*
> - *in some situations designers identify opportunities to design new products, places and communications;*
> - *in most situations designers are informed as to what needs designing, but they often challenge their brief to improve the solution;*
> - *designers need to take into consideration that their ideas will form part of a wider programme of investment, retail and marketing requirements.*

Investigating the context and identifying real needs

There is a danger of focusing too narrowly on the final product, place or communication being developed and so designers need to consider and understand the wider systemic context that the design challenge exists in. Sometimes a solution can be found by changing part of the system rather than an artefact within it.

Alongside the business or organization requirements it is critical that a professional designer identifies the physical and psychological needs of the users involved. To achieve this there are a range of established design methodologies, such as user research and user trials, cultural probes and obtaining ergonomic and anthropometric data, together with literature searches and seeking expert advice.

The most important skill however is perhaps that the designer is able to empathize with the potential stakeholders and users, and able to put themselves 'into their shoes', to identify and understand another's circumstances, feelings and desires, even though they might not necessarily agree with them. Empathy needs to centre on emotions and shared experiences: this usually involves careful listening and observing, enhanced by direct experience of the situation. A developed understanding of the micro-expressions of body language is needed: we are capable of perceiving an extraordinarily wide range of emotional responses just through observing subtle variations in a user's eyes. Empathy is mostly derived from the ability to recognize and interpret verbal and visual clues. There are many common empathetic words, and these can be grouped in different ways under various categories such as fear, anger, disgust, sadness, happiness and surprise, and ranked by intensity.

Designers also develop and use fictional 'Personas', or 'Lifestyle studies' to build up a composite picture of the needs and wants, behaviours and aspirations of a particular target market. These are usually derived from established data or adapted to the specific situation. The Persona can be developed under headings such as interests and values, media consumption, recreational activities and future goals, alongside a description of a typical day. Ideally the persona will include visual references to stylistic preferences for everyday products and environments. Meanwhile designers need to be fluent in the psychological application of the visual language, both to communicate ideas and to shape a user's experience.

At the same time the way something feels, sounds and smells are also essential ingredients in establishing the way in which the user will interact with a design and the overall feeling of satisfaction or frustration that will result.

At the same time the history of design provides rich insights into how designers design and the social, cultural and economic circumstances in which they operate. Professional designers understand that most design is evolutionary rather than revolutionary. In order to move forwards one has to have some awareness of where one has come from. Finding out about the previous solutions to the problem being tackled can often lead to important insights.

Such investigations of context and need usually result in a 'design specification', which define what is fixed and what can and needs to be determined by the designer. In practice there is usually flexibility in such specifications, and resolving the conflicts that occur within the specification forms a fundamental challenge.

> In design education students need to acquire the knowledge that:
> - artefacts exist and work within a system and context, not just as individual items;
> - designers can gain insights by trying to experience the difficulties involved in a problem for themselves;
> - designers need to empathise with potential users and stakeholders in order to identify what people really need and want, not just what they think or might say they need or want;
> - designers use or develop 'personas' to help understand user needs and wants in the context of their broader 'lifestyle' ;
> - 'aesthetics' include the way in which a user experiences a design as a whole, not just visually;
> - useful information can also be gathered by consulting experts in the field and consulting secondary source material, such as books and the internet
> - there is much to learnt from studying the way in which today's products, places and communications have evolved over time;
> - a design specification flexibly defines what can and cannot be changed and clearly identifies the conflicting requirements.

Inspire Me!

As all designers know, good ideas don't just 'happen' - they need to be prompted, incubated, transformed, connected, forgotten about and re-discovered. Some sort of inspiration is needed that goes beyond a blank sheet of paper, or increasingly these days a blank computer screen. Designers spend a lot of time observing things around them and storing them away for later reference, either by memorizing them, sketching or taking photos. The history of design also provides examples of brilliant designs that can prove inspirational. And if their existing repository of ideas doesn't provide any starting points they will go out specially to search for things that already solve similar problems and explore how they might be suitably modified, creating things such as concept, mood and material sample boards as starting points for discussion.

Explaining the problem or an idea to others often somehow concentrates the mind into producing its own insights. Finally there's nothing like stepping away from the problem and going for a run, taking a shower, cooking a meal, etc., to ensure the mind gets on with the job in the background, suddenly presenting a brilliant idea when it's least expected. So-called 'Eureka' moments don't just happen but need to be carefully prepared for and nurtured. Things sometimes appear to happen by chance, but in reality the circumstances in which those chances are more likely to occur have been carefully engineered.

In design education students need to acquire the knowledge that:
- *designers use a variety of sources of inspiration including transforming and connecting existing made and natural solutions that are analogous to the problem being explored;*
- *brainstorming and classification techniques can be used to widen their understanding and scope of their ideas which are openly discussed with others not involved in the design;*
- *designing involves exploiting the possibilities of taking risks, facilitating chance and utilizing serendipity in their approach to encourage 'eureka' moments of insight;*
- *while sometimes an initial hazy idea can form the basis of a final solution, exploring a wide range of other possibilities can be extremely beneficial;*
- *designers are curious and inquisitive in exploring new possibilities, and are continually dis-satisfied with the world and their own work.*

Modelling things up

Professional designers develop high levels of modelling skills. While different professions might focus on a particular type of modelling - the use of mathematical symbols, musical notation or the written and spoken word, for example - designers potentially apply them all in the pursuit of a solution. They have learnt to make appropriate decisions about what type of model to use and whether to make it all or a part of it smaller, larger, simpler, more detailed, or in a different material or format in order to explore and test out an idea. Sketches and 3D models, either 'real' or virtual, often incorporate words and numbers in an attempt to represent reality more quickly and cheaply than creating the real thing each time their thinking moves on. It is rare for just one 'model' to be made, but there will be an extended sequence and variety of different types of model.

In design education students need to acquire the knowledge that:
- *the size and material of representational models can be changed;*
- *designers often substitute and manipulate a different kind of model, i.e. using words, numbers, sketches, symbols can be used instead of the real thing;*
- *models can be skeletal (wire-frame), constructional or organic, and can be real or computer-generated;*
- *models can be tested through personal evaluation, comments made by other members of the team, practical performance tests and tests and evaluation with potential users and shareholders;*

- *the nature and purpose of what will be termed the final prototype needs to be clearly identified, and the manner in which it is to be tested and evaluated.*

Communication
Brilliant solutions to design problems are of no value if they cannot be effectively communicated to others. Broadly speaking designers communicate at three different levels - to themselves and other designers, to potential users and other stakeholders, and to those who will make and implement the proposals at a technical level. Designers understand that different people require different information which often needs to be presented in different ways, and they embrace all potential media in order to achieve this, carefully matching the purpose of the message with the requirements of the audience. They are adept at identifying the key features of a design idea and persuasively communicating its benefits to the target audience. This often involves the ability to tell compelling stories about user experiences, design processes and potentially successful products.

In design education students need to acquire the knowledge that:
- *the purpose and audience of their communications needs to be carefully considered, depending on whether they need to be personal, public or technical;*
- *designers use a wide variety of media and presentation techniques to tell powerful and memorable stories about the problems they have been tackling, the way they solved them and the features and benefits of their ideas.*

Planning and Organization
Design work is complex and multi-faceted, and in a professional context needs to be undertaken within strict constraints of resources, especially finance and time. As a design idea develops many decisions are influenced by these two issues, which can be generous or demanding. Meanwhile it is unusual for a design to be handled by a single person but more often a team of designers, each with different roles and expertise. It is also likely that there are a range of design projects being handled at the same time. In this situation collaborative teamwork and careful planning and organization are essential if the commission is to be delivered on time and on budget.

In design education students need to acquire the knowledge that:
- *designers work within a series of constraints and need to develop a solution within the requirements of a budget and varying time-scales;*
- *designers need to be able to work independently and also collaborate successfully with each other and with their clients.*

Evaluation
Designers continuously test and evaluate their processes and ideas, along with the designs of others. Comparing and contrasting the successes and failures of existing solutions often leads to important insights. They use a mixture of objective and subjective criteria involving observation, opinion and performance tests

to establish which ideas to reject and which to modify and explore further. This involves a high level of critical vocabulary and aesthetic judgement along with the ability to interpret data, and to question the accuracy and appropriateness of the results.

There are also social, cultural and moral issues to consider, and increasingly those of sustainability.

> *In design education students need to acquire the knowledge that:*
> - *there are differences between subjective and objective tests and comparing and contrasting existing designs;*
> - *designers develop a high level of critical verbal and visual vocabulary*
> - *different people have different aspirations, beliefs and values that need to be considered;*
> - *the current 'throw-away' approach to consumerism is unsustainable in the long-term.*

Knowledge Transfer

The main purpose of design education is not, as many seem to currently think, to produce the next generation of professional designers and engineers. The methodologies involved are eminently transferable across many disciplines and areas of life in which complex, open-ended problem-solving takes place, even though the participants may not recognize themselves as, or be called, 'designers'. Design education also develops and promotes the skills of self-directed individual learning.

Meanwhile many people at some stage become involved in projects that require the services of a designer and having a good knowledge of what can be achieved and the processes involved is extremely useful: many products that fail are often the result of uninformed and inadequate communication between the client and designer. Furthermore a well-informed, discerning consumer helps drive the market for well-designed goods that are found to be useful and satisfying to own.

Back to the Future (again)

A knowledge and experience of design and designing is far from exclusive to the subject of Design & Technology as currently specified and taught in schools, and Design education seems unlikely to thrive and prosper within it in the near future. Design education needs to find new homes in disciplines such as Design Thinking, the Digital Maker Movement, IT and STEAM, along with a new generation of teachers drawn from a wide sphere of approaches to open-ended problem-solving that are not limited to specific resistant material technologies. There is also a need for teachers of Art & Design to re-claim the teaching of design and craft that they largely relinquished during the 1990s.

The general aims of design education that emerged during the 1960s and 70s remain as important as ever in preparing children to live, learn and work in the 21st Century.

3.6 Design Thinking: What is it and where might it reside?
David Spendlove, Professor of Education, University of Manchester

Recently I was invited to attend the Global Teacher Prize awards in Dubai, which is probably the most lavish event in the education calendar. An indication of just how extravagant the occasion was can be demonstrated by Andrea Bocelli being the warm up act; Bear Grylls skydiving out of an aeroplane to deliver the trophy for which the winner was announced from the International Space Station and then the award was presented by Sheikh Mohammed bin Rashid Al Maktoum.

Preceding the award of the $1Million teacher prize was a two-day conference where some of the 'who's who' (and interlopers like myself) of the education world shared information and debated whilst ministers of education and dignitaries from around the world negotiated deals in the opulent surrounds of the Atlantis hotel. During the conference Andresa Schleicher, Head and coordinator of the OECD Programme for International Student Assessment (PISA) and considered as one the most influential experts in education, gave a keynote presentation in which he identified 'Design Thinking' as one of the five key areas promoting economic growth and social progress as part of the transformation of education.

Now, if you know a little about PISA and Andreas Schleicher then you will recognize both as being primarily orientated towards traditional educational disciplines and heavily dependent upon data measurements. And this is what made the announcement about design thinking all the more surprising as at present design thinking appears to be entering the everyday vernacular of the education world without there being any real consensus as to what it is, certainly not how it could be measured within an educational context or where it should be located within a curriculum.

Likewise the area of the curriculum in England, Design and Technology, that could be considered as the most closely associated with 'Design Thinking', is far from being regarded as central to transforming education. In fact Design and Technology is suffering an unprecedented and spectacular collapse and contraction to the extent it is in danger of almost being wiped out of the curriculum in some schools. So we have a paradox, in that whilst parts of the world appear to be embracing an emergent dimension of design education; in England a set of intentional and unintentional consequences seem to be perpetuating a rapid stifling of the curriculum area that potentially should offer a significant contribution to design thinking. This is even more ironic when it is recognized that England has been instrumental, for the last fifty years, in the international development of both the practice and research into design education. Yet a traditionalist focussed government schools minister; a narrowing of the curriculum; a marginalization of creative activities; a shortage of teachers and a funding crisis would suggest that the emergence of design thinking through the resuscitation of design and technology is highly unlikely if the present circumstances are maintained. However this may not all be bad news and here's why.

Design thinking is frequently and increasingly articulated and characterized as a rational, causal and logical approach, reducing a complex processes of design into a condensed, contrived and functional series of steps. In these circumstances I would characterise such activities as the antithesis of design thinking as they are more closely aligned with the dysfunctional and contrived model of 'design process' and assessment method that has contributed significantly to the downfall of Design and Technology in schools. Such reductive 'design processes' which can 'apparently' be applied to 'anything' severely distorts designing as a complex, intellectual activity, and even worse is used to drive assessment systems which have absurdly been adopted and used to define design capability through adherence to an artificial and highly contrived 'McDonaldsisation' of designing.

Likewise defining design thinking as a series of 'iterations', another term that is misunderstood, along a linear path merely conceives a potentially complex, intellectual, metacognitive and reflective activity as a formulaic, contrived, quasi-designing process. Such codification of design is unfortunately used to present designerly activities as a package that is transportable to different sectors and inevitably, like fast food can be attractive in its simplicity but lacking in its fulfilment. Despite or perhaps because of the perpetuation of reductive models of design thinking there appears to be a significant gaining of traction for the use of the term 'design thinking' in business, commerce, technology and education. When I do hear the term mentioned I generally ask the person using the term 'what do they mean' when they say 'design thinking' and do they just mean 'design' or do they just mean 'thinking'? The point being that in creating an open compound word from two words a new unit of meaning for design thinking must offer something different and add an alternative value to the individual words.

In considering this further, design thinking is also offering something to Nigel Cross's concept of 'design as a way of knowing'. As such design thinking offers an alternate mode of design enquiry, where enquiry of the mode and the epistemological basis of the enquiry are scrutinized and reflected upon in a cyclical manner (you might just want to read that sentence again). In this mode of thinking, we move away from conventional wisdom, notional common sense and tacit prepositions. We also move away from traditional concepts of product, artefact and aesthetic celebrity orientated design and become more human, earth and sustainability centred. Equally we move beyond form and function as a legitimate reductionist approach to expansive notions of what might be achieved through sustained designerly thinking and reflection.

Central to identifying what design thinking might be is challenging the epistemological basis of this embryonic, overly adopted and heavily distorted term. For this I am drawing upon my previous writing where I have explored how our emotions and sub-conscious processing plays a central part in our decision-making and how concepts of narcissism and altruism also influence our thinking. In previous writing I have also acknowledged that underlying assumptions relating to social, political, theological, psychological, philosophical and cultural values all interact with the decisions we each make. As such the overcoming of potentially restrictive heuristic flaws and the debiasing of such potential cognitive limitations through metacognitive and reflective approaches should be considered as central to design thinking.

Don Norman has suggested that new forms of design draw upon 'applied social and behavioural sciences and require understanding of human cognition and emotion, sensory and motor systems.' In such circumstances we draw upon multiple sources to better understand who and what we are designing for and seek a more sophisticated understanding of what design can offer. As such my view of design thinking is that it is more purposeful, sophisticated and complex than the traditional, broad definitions of design, using higher forms of thinking.

However, whilst I am trying to locate what design thinking might be I am also considering if and where it may exist within the school curriculum. One potentially obvious place is within design and technology but design and technology doesn't have a right to claim the design thinking territory, albeit it could be claimed that it does have a head start on other areas of the curriculum. Therefore in signalling that there are grounds to be optimistic about the future of a design and technology then this is on the basis of design thinking existing within a future model of design and technology rather than the current version of the subject. As such if we consider the current prevailing model of design and technology in schools to be conceived of as design and technology version 1.0 we can then recognise version 1.0 may be coming to the end of its lifespan. Whilst we could also go into the nuances in that we might be currently operating on version 1.5 or 1.6, for now we can say that 1.0 characterizes a model of delivery that enjoyed incredible success, at times, but that given some of the circumstances outlined, is now coming to the end of its lifecycle. Therefore there is a need to conceive of a new form of design and technology, which I would posit, should be 'Design and/or Technology 2.0'.

In positing the emergence of 'Design and/or Technology 2.0' there is now an opportunity to consider the contribution of design thinking in an education context. More specifically there is an opportunity to consider design thinking as the catalyst for the next version of 'Design and/or Technology 2.0'. Adoption of design thinking into a new model of design and technology will not however be straightforward given the existence of the difficulties that traditional notions of design have had in becoming established in practice in the 1.0 version. This is why design thinking has to be situated in a new model of design and technology. Nevertheless the emergence of design thinking could, and in fact already is, be gaining a foothold in other parts of the curriculum, such as humanities or science and it will be up to the design and technology community to show the same tenacity as was apparent in the emergence of design and technology 1.0 in order to capitalise on a window of opportunity for embracing design thinking.

Ultimately we have the intersection of the rapid demise of design and technology 1.0 and the spectacular rise of design thinking, albeit in its ill-defined and unadopted form. There is therefore a unique, perhaps once in a decade, opportunity for reorientation of the values that were instrumental within the development of design and technology through adopting and capitalising upon the intellectual and reflective aspects of design thinking and re-visioning them within 'Design and/or Technology 2.0'. If the design and technology community are insufficiently proactive then we risk losing a generation of learners who will be bereft of an informed design literacy and the further demise of an underutilized and misunderstood subject that potentially still has huge amounts to offer in the broad education of all children.

4. EPISTEMOLOGY AND VISUAL THINKING

From the outset of this book the case has been made that meaning can be expressed through images as well as symbols and language. In his book, *Design: Models of Change*, Ken Baynes explains the potential of visual/spatial qualities; physical places, things and communications; and human values and meanings, as the beginnings of an epistemological structure for a visual language. A key passage is reproduced below.

> 'In the design field what kinds of 'equivalents' are required? Here is a selection of physical properties, aesthetic qualities and spatial relations that are difficult (or impossible) to convey in natural language:
>
> COLOUR
> SPACE
> FORM and SHAPE
> MOVEMENT
> STRUCTURE
> DISTANCE
> PROXIMITY
> TEXTURE
> PATTERN
> SPATIAL RELATIONSHIPS
> SCALE
> PROPORTION
> VISUAL RHYTHM
>
> To these essentially visual/spatial properties we could add those to do with sound/noise and, indeed, any properties of the natural or made world that impact on our senses and so on our minds and behaviour. For the designer these properties underlie and translate into the specific forms and constructions found in the made world:
>
> LANDSCAPES   TRANSPORT SYSTEMS
> TOWNSCAPES   VEHICLES
> TOWNS   CLOTHES
> VILLAGES   MACHINES
> HOUSES   EQUIPMENT
> PUBLIC BUILDINGS   ENTERTAINMENT MEDIA
> SHOPS   GRAPHIC IMAGES
> PRODUCTS

A further list would move from physical things, places and communications to deal with qualities which people might value in those things, places and communication:

PRIVATE	METROPOLITAN
CONVENIENT	RURAL
BEAUTIFUL	HIGH-SPEED
EXCITING	RELAXING
IDENTITY	GLOBAL
TRADITIONAL	LOCAL
FASHIONABLE	GREEN
MODERN	RESPONSIVE
PROGRESSIVE	COMMUNAL
COST EFFECTIVE	CLEAR
PURPOSE-BUILT	SIMPLE
HOME MADE	EASY TO USE

These lists only provide a preliminary sketch of essentially non-verbal aspects of design activity and awareness. Notice how each word evokes a visual response. 'Town' has one slide-show in the mind; 'village' a related but quite different one. 'Exciting' has one visual range; 'tranquil' another. The imagery at play deploys qualities from the first list: 'colour', 'form', 'movement' etc. The intention here is to highlight the interconnectedness of three different visual 'languages' that can be used in designerly thinking:

VISUAL/SPATIAL QUALITIES
PHYSICAL PLACES, THINGS and COMMUNICATIONS
HUMAN VALUES AND MEANINGS

It would be easy to construct a matching list of negative qualities – which for some people might also include some of those listed above as positives! Notice how difficult it would be to deal with them completely using natural language alone. It is necessary to be able to say 'look, it could be like this' or 'see, these are the traditional colours' or 'I'll take the lid off the model – then you can try out how easy it would be to change the batteries." (Baynes, 2013: 101-102).

Ken Baynes' contribution to this volume in Section 4.1, 'Meaning without words', extends this discussion primarily using a visual format.

Embracing knowledge that has been expressed in visual format seems to have either eluded the attention of writers concerned with design epistemology or proved problematic, and consequently some possible starting points from Xenia Danos' research have been included in Section 4.2. Her contribution relates to taking systematic approaches to studying graphicacy as expressed in still, visual images in educational contexts. Danos' taxonomy, derived from Fry's, provides an approach to categorizing graphicacy, and her presentation of research by Gaitskell, Lowenfeld and Kellogg suggests the beginnings of a framework for understanding the development of graphicacy skills. Getting to grips with design epistemology will require systematic approaches to the expression of meanings through graphicacy, and as that discussion extends to general education, then it must clearly engage with the development of graphicacy skills in humans.

Blackwell & Engelhard (1998) identified a number of taxonomies of images (called diagrams by the authors), which embodied significant diversity. They also proposed 6 taxonomic dimensions in order to develop a 'taxonomy of taxonomies' as follows:

> 'i. **The representation - the graphic display:** Describes the organisation of the display - distribution of ink and colour. It tends to identify different components, and their relationships
>
> ii. **The message - the represented information**: Informational structure (graphical structure) is defined in terms of the relationships present in the data.
>
> iii. **Relation between representation and message**: As a sign system, the diagram signifies information that is related to its graphic structure; defining a correspondence between the graphical structure and its interpretation. The correspondence may also require interpretation beyond simple mapping of structure, varying with the extent to which it is pictorial, or the extent to which it involves structural analogy.
>
> iv. **Task and process (interpreting and modifying representations):** In a taxonomy that considers how the diagram is used (a science of thinking-with-diagrams rather than simply a science of diagrams), the processes of construction and interpretation must also be considered. Some of these processes are "internal" cognitive processes, while some appear to depend completely on physical devices or tools. In fact, processes of diagram use form a continuum of physical and cognitive operations which is divided only at the peril of the taxonomist. Some taxonomies emphasise particular portions of this continuum (ergonomics, or mental reasoning), but we include them all here.
>
> v. **Context and convention (cultural and communicative context):** The way that we interpret depictive conventions depends on cultural context as well as the conventions of particular media types.
>
> 6. **Mental representation (diagrams in the head):** Mental representation and the static properties of mental representations.'
>
> (Blackwell & Engelhard, 1998, 2-3)

Blackwell and Engelhardt did not mention Fry's taxonomy of graphs (1974), but the taxonomic dimensions help to focus attention on particular aspects. According to Fry his taxonomy was designed to be useful for teaching and testing graphs knowledge in the government-funded schools and in helping writers and readers in many communication media, including journals, textbooks, popular press, computer graphics, and television. Fry's taxonomy was the most appropriate for Xenia Danos' research in an educational context, but she found that it needed updating. Its updating and validation are described here.

Blackwell and Engelhardt saw the development of taxonomies of images as an on-going process and Xenia Danos sees her taxonomy as a work-in-progress. The significant point here is that systematic approaches to the consideration of graphicacy can be made and further developed.

References

Baynes K (2013) *Design: Models of Change: the impact of designerly thinking on people's lives and the environment* , Loughborough Design Press, Shepshed

Blackwell F & Engelhard A (1998) 'A Taxonomy Of Diagram Taxonomies'. In *Proceedings Of Thinking With Diagrams 98: Is There A Science Of Diagrams?*, 60–70

Fry E (1974) 'Graphical Literacy', cited in *Journal Of Reading*, 1981, 24 (5), 383-390

4.1 Meanings without words
Ken Baynes

THE SHAPE OF IDEAS

Any claim for the importance of Graphicacy will need first to demonstrate that the brain is capable of making visual meaning as well as modelling visual perceptions. In our culture, cognition is strongly associated with words and numbers. Yet our culture is also the most visual that has so far existed. Notice, for example, that even words and numbers take on graphic form when they are written.

These days the dominant mode of communication is to use words and images together, often with an accompanying sound track. This happens throughout popular culture in graphic novels, film, television, computer games and social media.

So, I decided to use words and images in comic book mode to explore what is unique to graphic meaning and how it differs from other ways of making meaning.

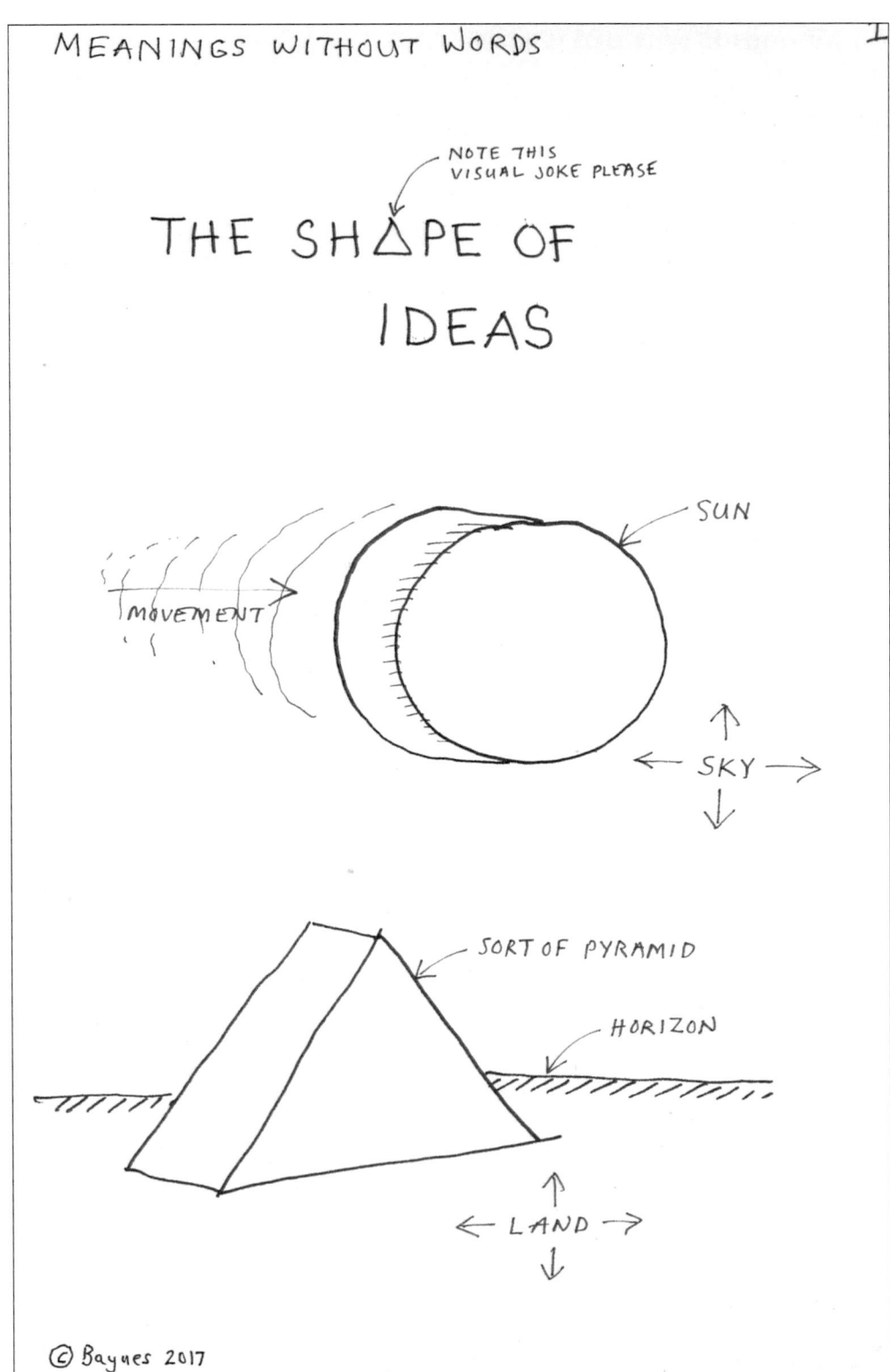

Figure 4.1

Figure 4.2

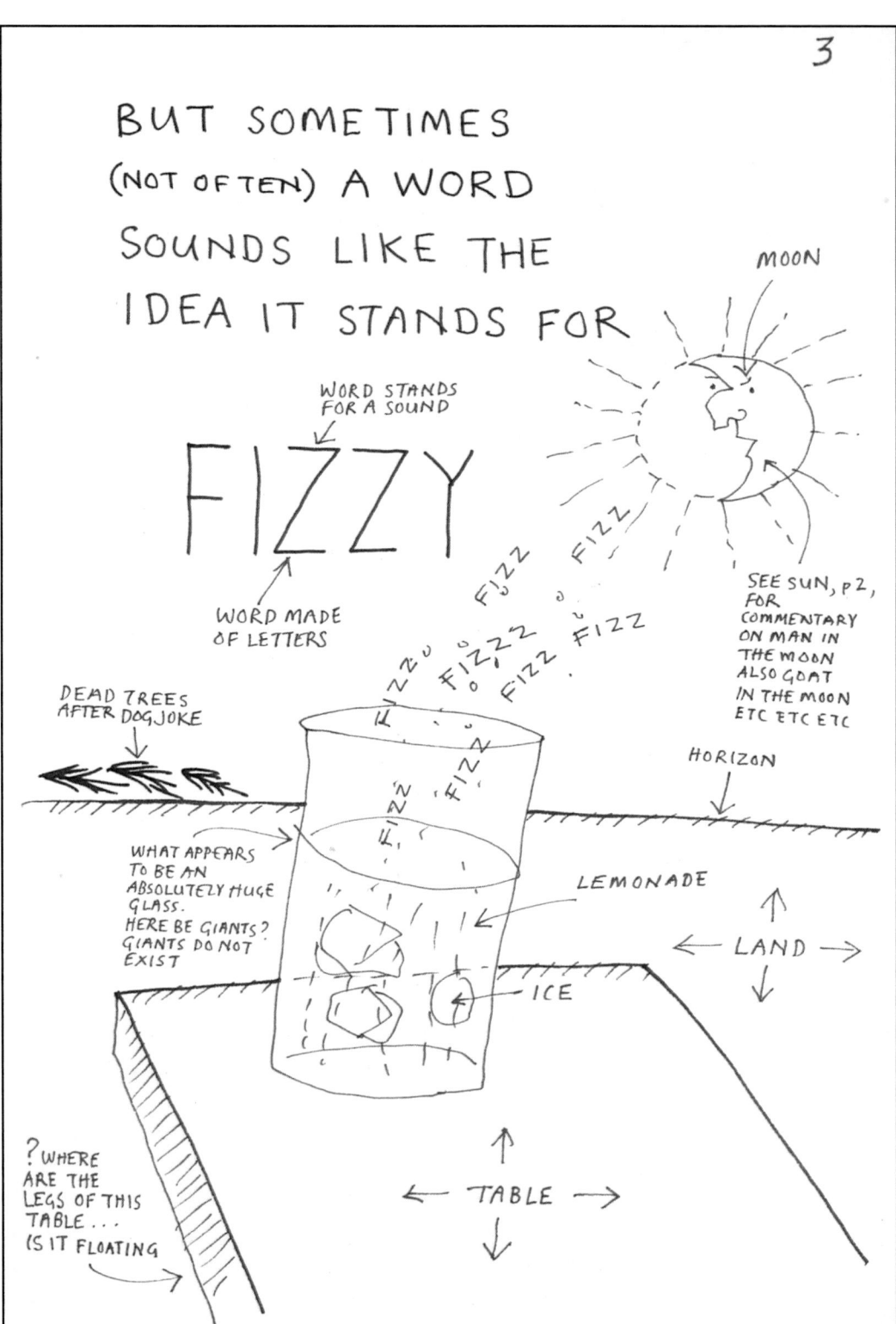

Figure 4.3

WHAM!

Although words take on graphic form when they are written, you cannot simply use words to do the job of a picture (or vice versa). The world of sounds can be suggested in spoken language and graphics – WHAM, SPLAT, PITTER, PATTER. This is fun but no substitute for an ear-splitting reality. Graphic imagery – a painting for example – only shows one aspect of experience: it shows you how things look not how they feel, smell or sound.

We all understand something about the potential and limitations of different media but we usually take them for granted. In thinking about how we know what we know it is important to stop taking them for granted.

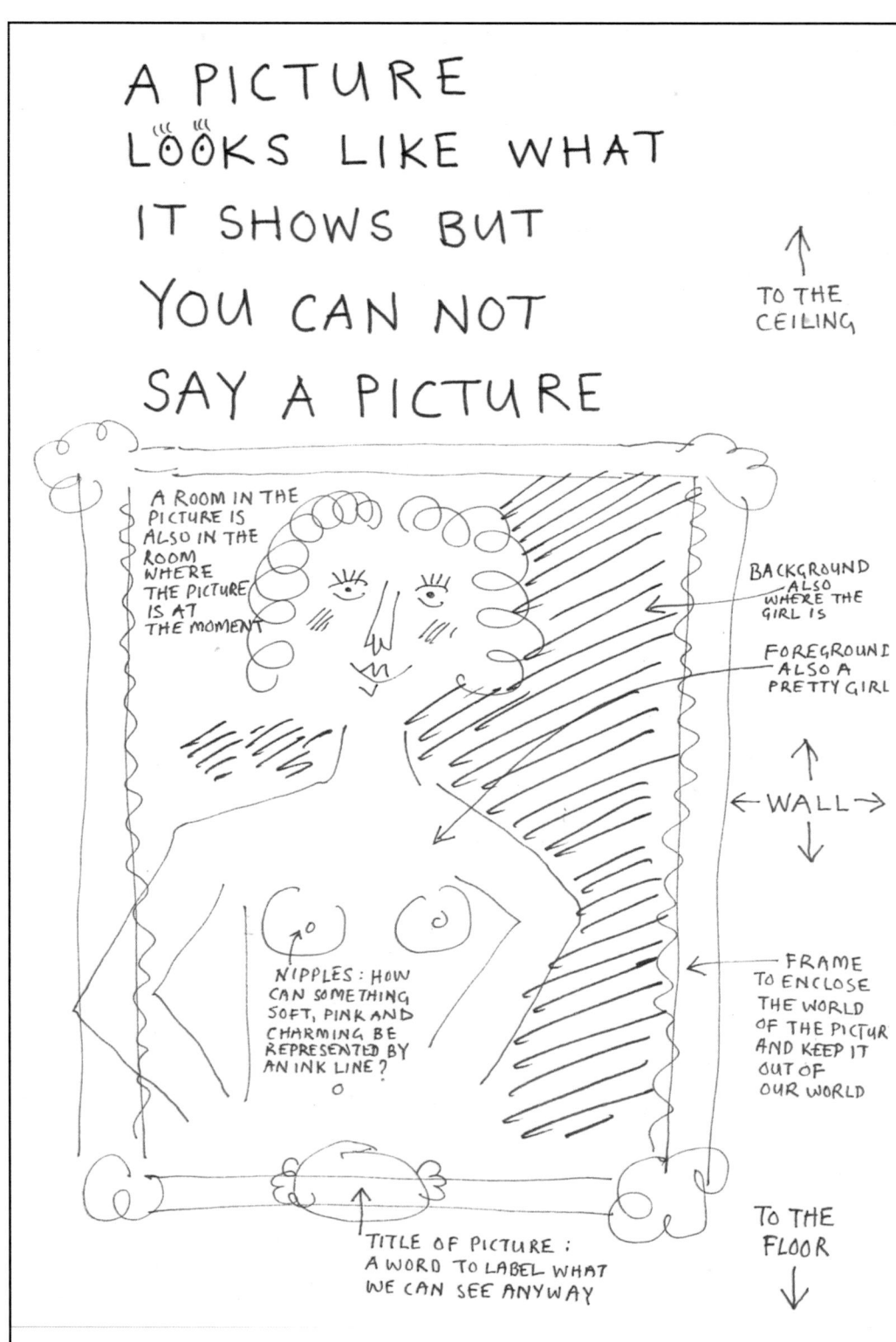

Figure 4.4

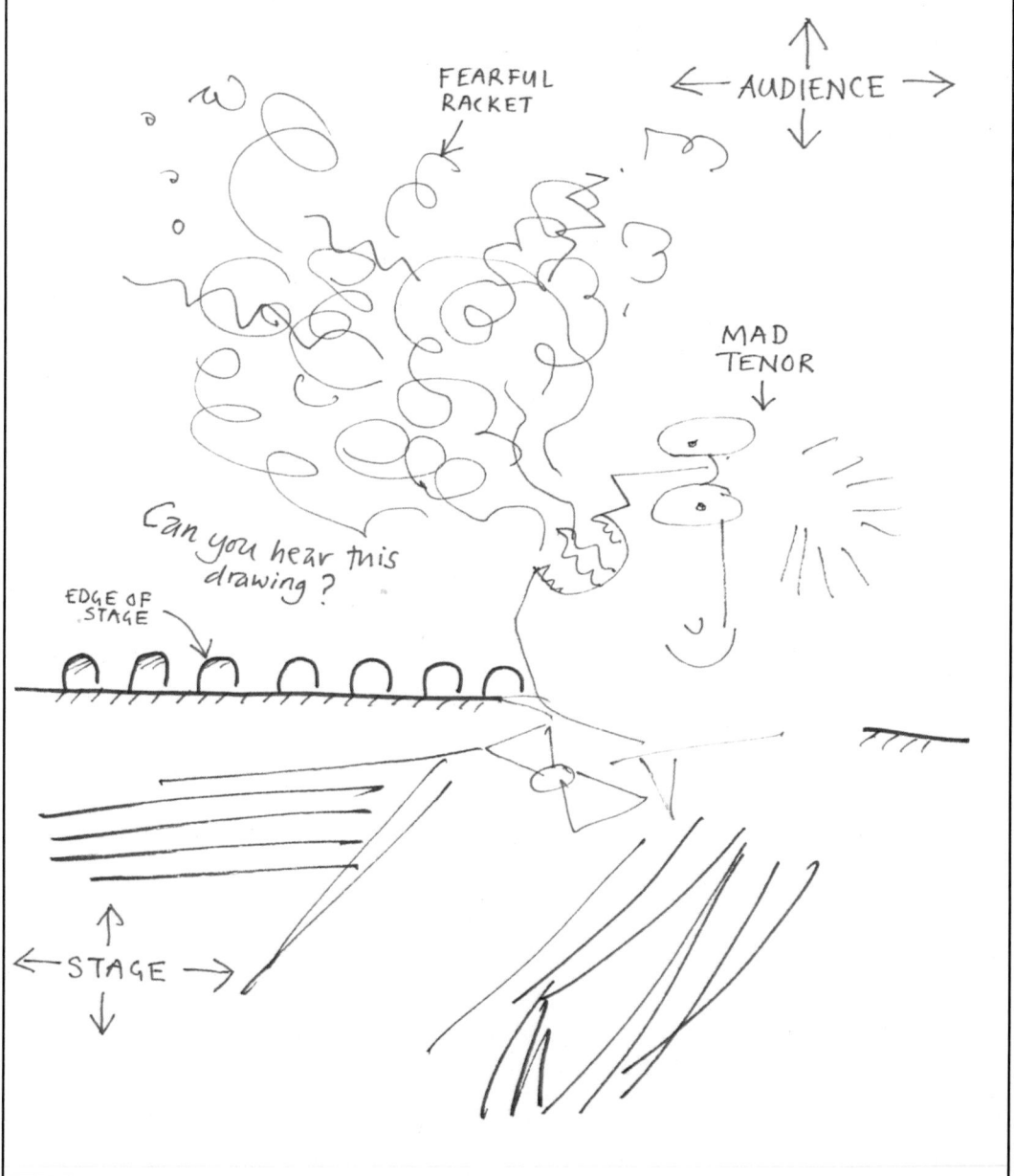

Figure 4.5

MODELS 'R' US

Can you hear this drawing? Of course not, yet an image can evoke a response from all our senses, not just vision. Equally a sound can spark imagery. In extreme form this is called 'synaesthesia' but we all experience it to some extent. It is yet another way in which the mind can make creative connections.

Our mind is constantly refining its understanding of sense data: our experience of reality comes from models that the mind has built from experience. These models are 'us'. It is these models that we use to link past, present and future. These models enable us to design things.

What is seen in the 'mind's eye' is in dynamic relationship both with perception and actions in and on the world. Note: something really CLEVER is going on here.

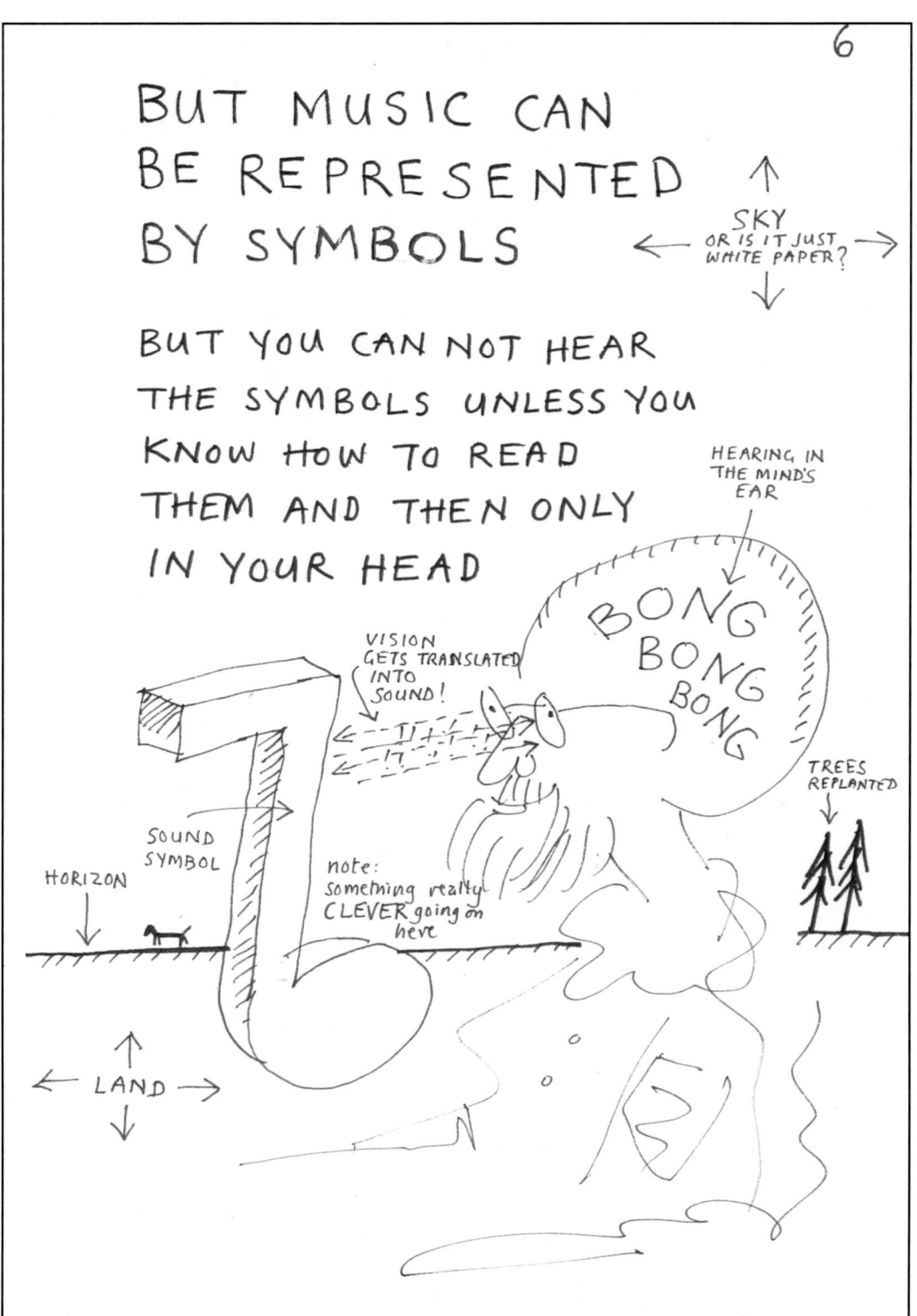

Figure 4.6

IN PRAISE OF DOODLES

I am a great believer in the power of doodling. Doodles and swift sketches are to be celebrated. It is quite remarkable how a few marks can capture complex meanings – scientific theories, aesthetic ideas, designs, a landscape, engineering principles. A purposeful doodle is a powerful conceptual tool.

Famous sketches include Charles Darwin's little doodle of a twig- like structure annotated with the words 'I think'. Here in eight or so marks was the essence of evolution as a branching tree of species. Or Walt Disney's first scratchy versions of Mickey Mouse. Here was the starting point of one of the world's greatest media empires. Or Leonardo's marginal sketch of a helicopter – a concept that existed before technology and science actually made it possible.

 A simple mark is full of potential for the future.

Paul Klee was the master of scribble and mark-making. His use of marks to tell stories and illuminate aesthetic ideas makes him one of the great artists of the Twentieth century.

TAKING A LINE FOR A WALK

Taking a line for a walk is a beguiling exercise. Primary school children get the idea at once. Unlike adults, they find imaginary journeys easy to make. Taking a line for a walk is story-telling without words.

PAUL KLEE's Thoughts on Drawing TAKE US FOR A WALK IN THE COUNTRY. WE START (of course) FROM

• A POINT

THIS EXTENDS TO GIVE US A LINE, OUR ROUTE THROUGH THIS WORLD OF DRAWING

WE STOP ONCE OR TWICE

WE CROSS A RIVER BY BOAT ...

AND A PLOUGHED FIELD

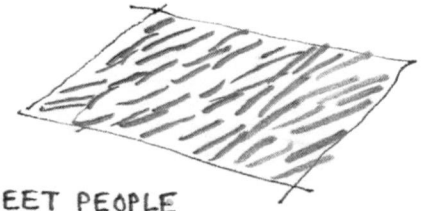

WE MEET PEOPLE BASKETMAKERS COMING HOME IN THEIR CART

THEY HAVE A CHILD WITH FUNNY CURLS

Figure 4.7

THE WEATHER BECOMES SULTRY AND LOWERING. THERE IS A FLASH OF LIGHTENING

THERE ARE SOON STARS OVERHEAD

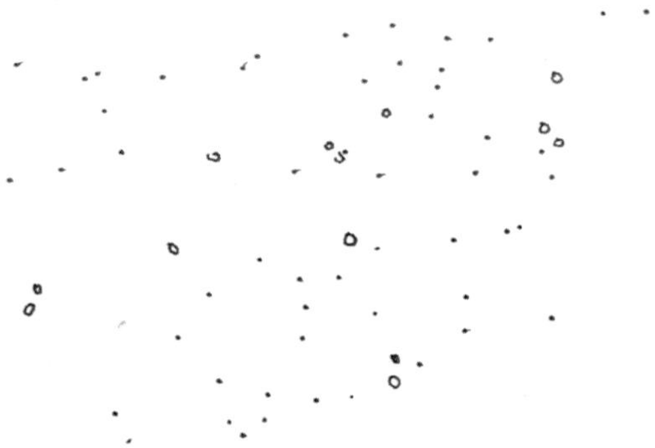

THE DAY COMES TO AN END

"Before we fall asleep, we remember our journey. It was rich in impressions. All kinds of different lines. Blobs of colour. Stippling. Stipled and striped surfaces. Undulatory movement. Broken, articulated movement. Counter-movement. Objects interlaced and inter-woven ... Harmony with one voice"

– PAUL KLEE, 1918.

Figure 4.8

Figure 4.9

LOST FOR WORDS

Examples of ideas that cannot be properly explained in words were given at the start of this chapter under the headings:

VISUAL/SPATIAL QUALITIES
PHYSICAL PLACES, THINGS and COMMUNICATIONS
HUMAN VALUES AND MEANINGS

Here are some further examples:

- a person's face or the colour of their hair;

- a patchwork of green fields;

- a plan for a new town;

- the face of the moon.

Words and numbers can play a part in describing or measuring these things but only graphic models can capture the experience and the visual reality.

GRAPHIC THOUGHTS

As with written language or numbers, graphic imagery makes it possible for us to think thoughts and model ideas that cannot be explored in any other way. The next three pages highlight the conceptual power of a line.
A line can transform a page into a theatre for observations and ideas, an arena in which to explore aesthetic qualities or a window into space so that we seem to look beyond and through the paper surface.

These three capacities helped to create the modern world. Starting with perspective and map-making in the Renaissance, they developed through observational drawing in anatomy, astronomy and through the microscope to completely transform humanity's view of itself and the natural environment. In the industrial revolution, images played a key role in invention and design and in communicating scientific and technological principles.

Now the use of lines for exploration, design and communication has grown exponentially. Along with other visual qualities, and the magnifying power of digital media, we have a powerful cognitive and affective realm at our disposal. It would be wise to become more fluent in its language.

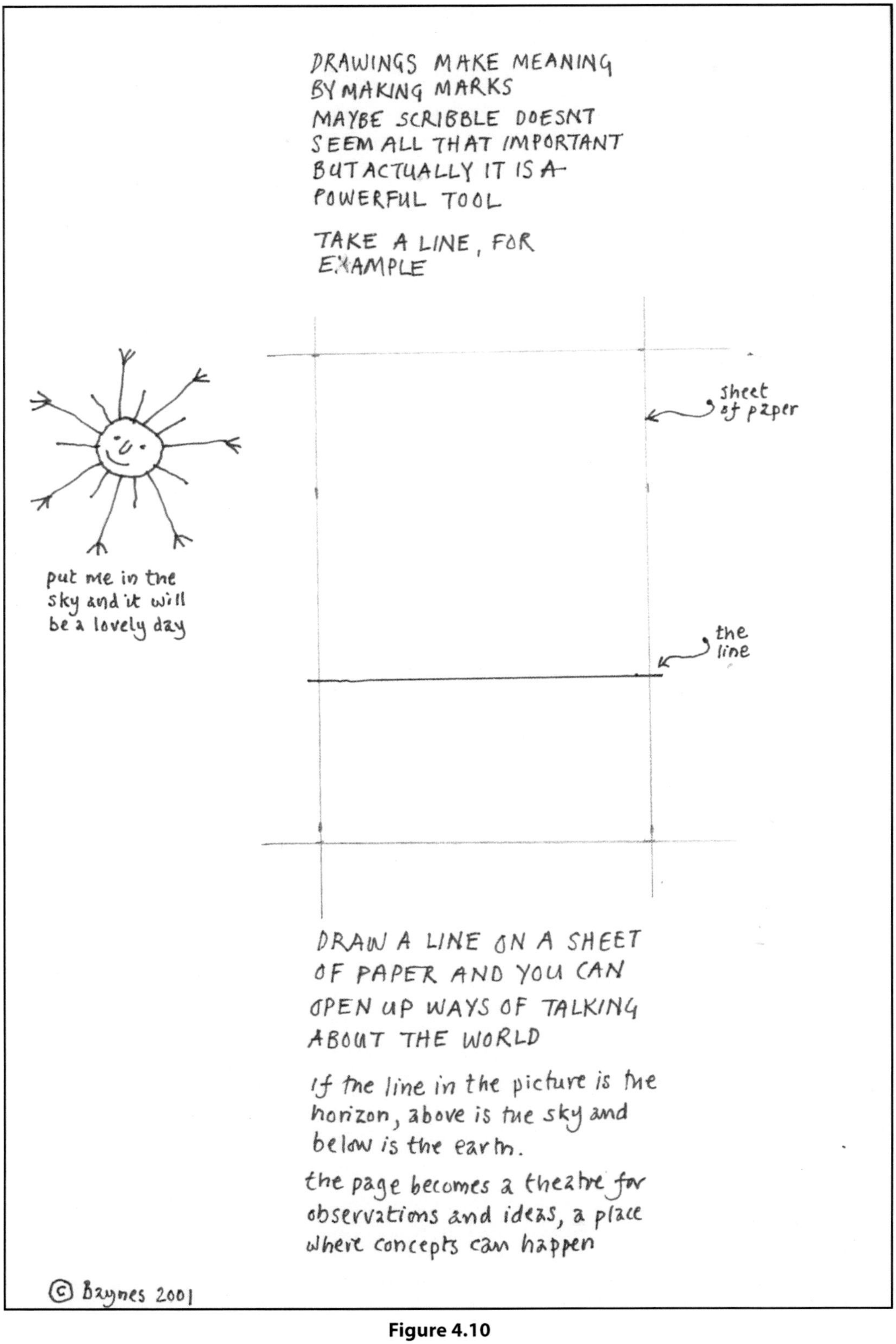

DRAWINGS MAKE MEANING
BY MAKING MARKS
MAYBE SCRIBBLE DOESNT
SEEM ALL THAT IMPORTANT
BUT ACTUALLY IT IS A
POWERFUL TOOL

TAKE A LINE, FOR
EXAMPLE

← sheet of paper

put me in the sky and it will be a lovely day

← the line

DRAW A LINE ON A SHEET
OF PAPER AND YOU CAN
OPEN UP WAYS OF TALKING
ABOUT THE WORLD

If the line in the picture is the horizon, above is the sky and below is the earth.

the page becomes a theatre for observations and ideas, a place where concepts can happen

© Baynes 2001

Figure 4.10

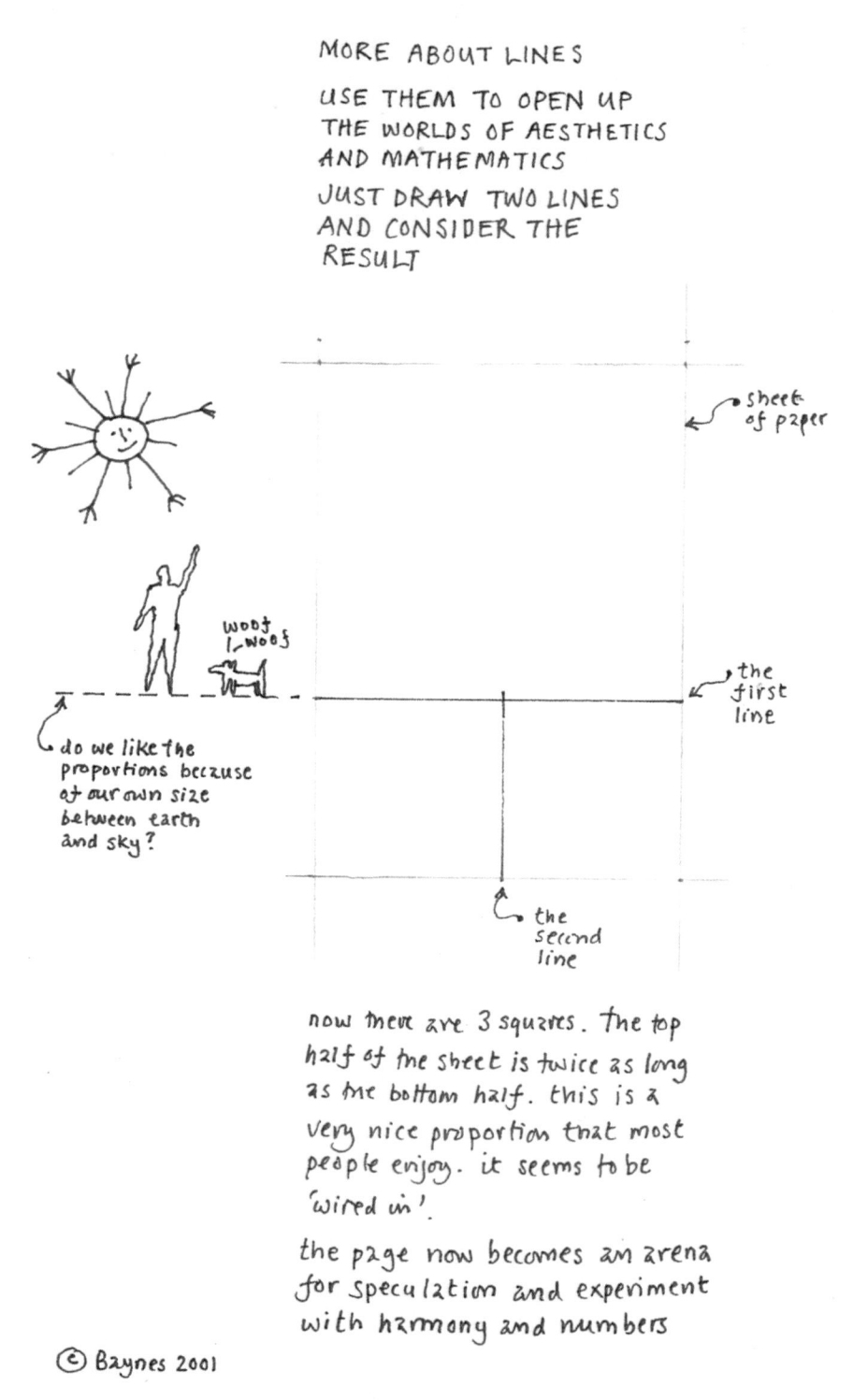

Figure 4.11

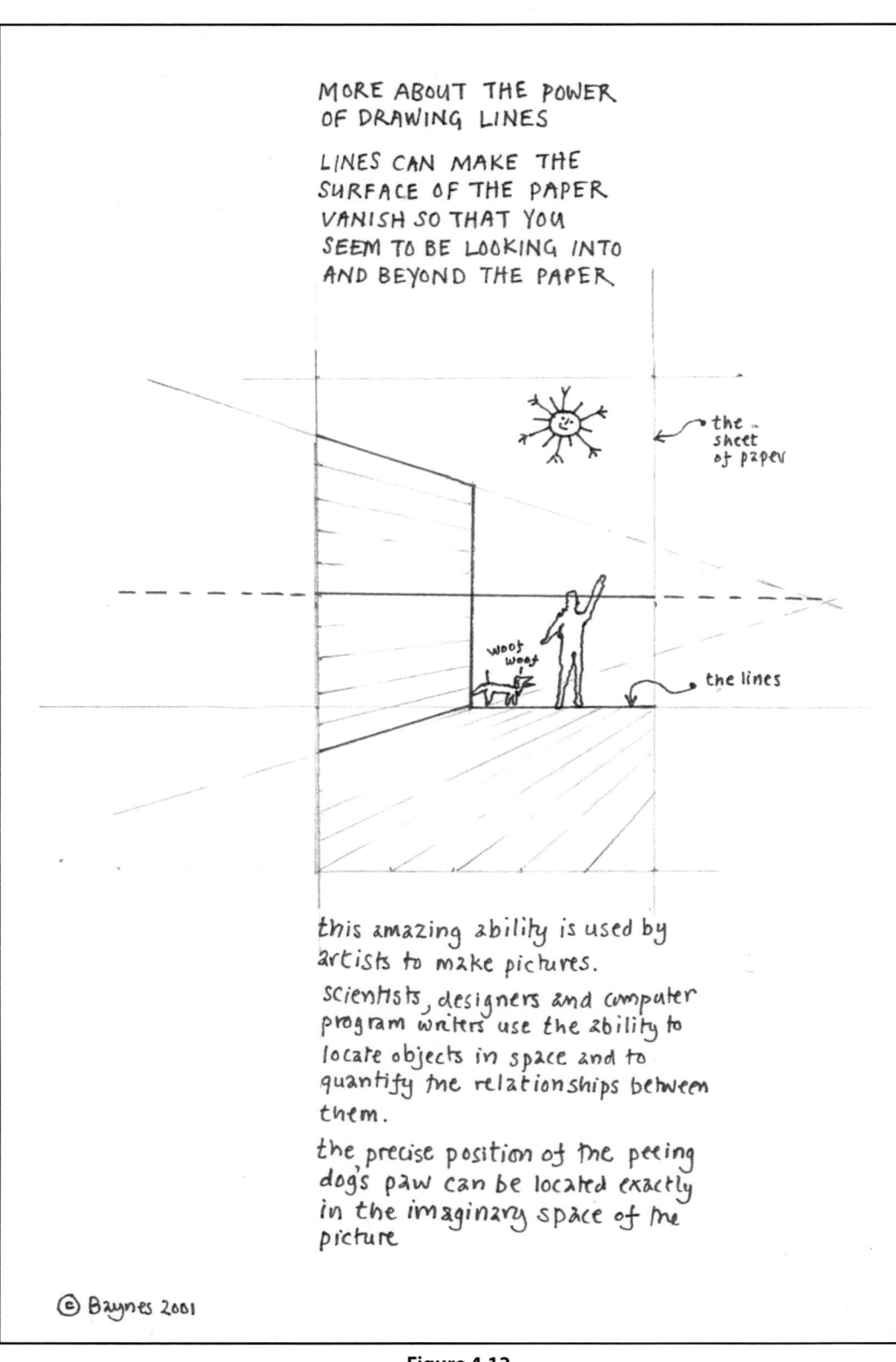

Figure 4.12

4.2 GRAPHICACY AND A TAXONOMY

Xenia Danos, Education Officer and Research Co-ordinator, KES College, Nicosia, Cyprus

Introduction

Graphicacy is one of the first innate communication skills developed in humans, and the only one – when compared with numeracy and literacy – which develops naturally to a satisfactory level, enabling communication. Children, primarily develop graphicacy skills through their innate curiosity, need for experimentation and play.

Graphicacy is a complex cognitive process, which entails a sequence of events. The level of accuracy and detail with which each one is completed, has a direct impact on the quality of the outcome. The sequence includes the following: observing an idea, a feeling, a sequential happening, 3-dimensional objects – beings – landscape etc; processing the information of what is to be communicated by making links, connections, identifying special features etc in the 'mind's eye'; and using drawing techniques, translating and communicating the information by making marks i.e. creating an image.

In general, humans develop graphicacy skills naturally to a degree. Research has mapped the age range and stages children go through, starting from 6 months to 8 years of age. These usually reach a point where children can communicate through symbolic representations, and can be fairly impulsively driven, such as a simple outline drawing of a sun made in the sand using a stick. Through nurture however, we can develop much more complex graphicacy skills, such as the ability to create read and understand elaborate engineering drawings demonstrating the relationships and functions of multiple items working together, such as the parts of a steam engine.

Near the time numeracy and literacy is introduced to children in schools, the natural development of graphicacy skills starts subsiding. Children have to begin to make an effort to further develop their graphicacy skills. While observing and learning from their environment, children are faced with a culture which actively promotes a narrow and direct focus on the importance of literacy and numeracy. Graphicacy related tasks such as drawing, are often portrayed as of lesser value when dealing with learning, progression and academic achievements after the age of 8.

It is clearly demonstrated that graphicacy is relevant in many areas of education, with a strong significance for specific subject areas, such as design and design education. This is because designing and understanding design involve the use of mental and physical models, many of which are essentially visual (Baynes, 2013:6). Baynes states that:

'… much modelling in the mind (designerly thinking) is extended through graphic models. The fluent use and understanding of visual media and understanding of the visual/spatial content of the designed environment are amongst the active ingredients of a design culture.'

Fully analyzing and describing the relationship between design education and graphicacy is work that is yet to be completed.

As long ago as 1965, Balchin and Coleman (1965:85) were arguing that 'graphicacy' should be a recognized part of general education. In a memorable phrase, they described it as 'the fourth ace in the pack' along with oracy, numeracy and literacy. Since then there has been a striking increase in the use of visual means of communication both in education and society at large. In my own practice as a teacher and researcher, I have attempted both to develop a better understanding of the nature of graphicacy and to experiment with ways of teaching it (Danos, 2014). A central feature of my work is a taxonomy of graphicacy which I put forward as a useful tool for structuring the field and as a basis for further development.

In this article I set out to:

1. offer a definition of graphicacy;
2. illustrate the importance of graphicacy in society;
3. note that, by contrast, the teaching of graphicacy plays only a minor role in the curriculum;
4. present a preliminary identification of the categories and elements involved in graphicacy and identify the key incoming and outgoing skills relevant to graphicacy;
5. propose a taxonomy of graphicacy;
6. discuss the developmental stages involved in graphicacy;
7. show that graphicacy can be fostered by teaching and learning.

1. Definition of graphicacy

Graphicacy is the ability to communicate through still visual images, such as maps, diagrams, graphs and symbols (Danos, 2012). The cognitive requirements that accompany such skills, e.g. modelling 'in the mind's eye' and critical thinking, support activity in numerous fields. Important 'life skills' are introduced through education from an early age, using policies on literacy, numeracy and articulacy. Graphicacy, however, which is used extensively in the early years and later through school and beyond, has yet to be introduced through a strategic approach (Anning, 1997; Wilmot, 1999; Hope, 2008; Danos, 2012). Currently graphicacy does not explicitly feature in the structured curricula in England; this is similar in many other countries within Europe, the US and Australia, among others (Krane & Dyson, 1981; Balchin, 1996; Danos, 2012). The main reasons for this are believed to be the low significance attached to graphicacy skills for the development of an intellectually well-balanced human; and the high complexity level involved in analyzing and defining the areas of graphicacy, which are both related to a lack of research effort in this area (Fry, 1981; Danos, 2012).

2. Importance of graphicacy in society
Evidence of the importance of graphicacy skills for today's professionals and the acknowledgment of its existence on various levels can be found in the research conducted in numerous different countries, including Australia, South Africa, Ireland, the UK and the USA; many of which have asked for Balchin & Coleman's 1965 journal paper to be reprinted at some stage. This indicates the strength of the common ground surrounding the concept of graphicacy and its potential to support curriculum development.

The practical implementation of graphicacy across formal and established organizations forms another example; the European Commission is using standardised psychometric tests as one of their candidate selection procedures. This is comprised of verbal, numerical and abstract reasoning tests. Abstract reasoning (also known as conceptual reasoning) tests relate to visual pattern recognition through a series of abstract images measuring the ability to identify logical rules and trends in new data, the integration of this information, and its application in problem solving. To further support this view, literature has identified numerous other Intelligence Quotient (IQ) tests which use abstract reasoning tasks as part of their assessment, to measure or quantify the level of the participant's intelligence. There are also books which provide help for candidates to prepare and practise for such tests. These provide strong suggestions on how to enhance elements of graphicacy and give potential indications for aspects of continuity and progression relating to the main stages through which graphicacy capabilities can develop, as well as providing supporting evidence for the belief that graphicacy can be nurtured and developed.

> 'Images. They are so compelling that we cannot not watch them. They are so seductive that they have revolutionized human social communication. Oral and written communication are in decline because a new form of communication, communication by image, has emerged.' (Davis, 1992)

Even though the above statement has a strong element of drama and exaggeration, it provides an acute sense of the current situation. Davis mentions communication via images as a 'new form of communication', whereas others would see this as reverting back to our innate intelligence and cognitive strengths as humans. The history of human social interchange has evolved through four distinct phases: visual-symbolic representations, oral, text-based, and now again visual-image centered communication. From cave markings and paintings depicting scenes from everyday life, to the sharing of stories and traditions by word of mouth, allowing for cultures to be passed on and to grow. Later, writing was introduced, allowing for the stories to be grounded, preserving information with precision and consistency. With the passing of time, advertising has flourished, opening the space for visual communication to return, and this time targeting the influence of emotions. Technology has also evolved, introducing us to more direct ways of receiving such stimuli, and integrating them into popular culture.

> 'Making and interpreting marks, is, and has been, fundamental to all peoples and cultures. Drawing is extraordinarily versatile and has a huge repertoire of forms and uses. It is an intellectual activity that links sensing, feeling, thinking and doing' (Baynes, 2008).

When Baynes (2008) asked people from different professions the question 'why draw?', these were the key reasons given:

- it is an essential part of the work of imagining;
- constructing and managing production;
- to explore ideas;
- communicate key points to other people;
- highlight features;
- set out a structure;
- support calculations for technical details;
- planning and organizing.

In a world where information is often technical and time is often short, visual images potentially offer a direct, fast, effective and efficient way of communicating. Consequently as a society, and as the growth of the use of the Internet continues, where often websites use images and animations to support or bring forward messages, we are becoming ever more dependent on visual images.

> 'Our cultural references (are) becoming increasingly visually based. Society seems to be buoyant with smiling poo emojis, Instagram wellness shots and endless Adele memes. Some brands are responding to this change rapidly and successfully; we're even seeing it seeping into news reporting.'
> (*The Guardian*, 2016).

The use of images around us is clearly immense, to the point where we can easily become overwhelmed. Subliminal messages are passed onto us nonstop, shaping our thoughts, conditioning our perspective and influencing our emotions. It is now our duty, to learn and develop relevant graphicacy skills, allowing us to see through these interferences.

3. Importance of graphicacy in teaching and learning

Graphicacy is often seen by various 'more academic disciplines' as an inferior communication tool, and there is a tendency to place verbal and numerical communication as superior in their perception and education agendas. And yet, it is generally accepted and supported by research, amongst others, that images:

1. transmit information faster;
2. trigger emotions instantly;
3. enhance comprehension;
4. allow for the fast pattern recognition and the creation of links;
5. allow for new information to be placed in long term memory (remember it longer);
6. as well as inspiring and motivating people.

'We live in a visual world, a world which would collapse without its visual images. What has not yet happened in education, in general, is the full recognition of pictorial conceptualisation' (Krane & Dyson, 1981:21).

Fry (1981) maintains that isolated elements of graphicacy teaching exist in many schools but that it is not well developed or understood as a concept; an opinion shared also by Wilmot (1999). Aldrich and Sheppard (2000) noted that unlike literacy, graphicacy is rarely taught explicitly, despite being an important skill. Although the National Curriculum for primary science in England at Key Stage 1 (5-7 year-olds) states that children falling within this category should be able to present scientific information in a number of ways, through drawings, diagrams, tables and charts, and in speech and writing, on the whole its agenda regarding graphicacy is an implicit one. Children seem to be expected to 'pick it up as they go along'.

Independent research has explored the importance of graphicacy in education e.g. the balance of text-based and visually-based resources within educational materials and its importance for learning (Verdi et al. 1996; Pettersson 1993), the significance of graphicacy in the presentation of quantitative information in an educational context (Jones et al. 2000) and the emerging research agendas associated with computer generated images. For example, Ochaya (2005) conducted a study within an educational context which focused on the use of 3D graphics and animation software used to enhance learning. The results indicated that students, who used the interactive 3D graphic and animation instructional software, learned more easily and could work better under pressure.

It is often assumed that, during teaching, visual images enhance understanding and learning, especially where children of 'low abilities' are concerned. Some studies have however found that visual images might not always be the best means to aid teaching. Ausburn (1980) stressed the point that the same learners who have reading problems appear more likely to have problems in analyzing complex visuals. However, currently there is little information that explains what it is about the human mind that makes graphics and other pictorial displays more effective than other formats containing similar information (Pinker, 1985). Nevertheless, Finson and Pederson have a firm belief that images are invaluable in teaching. They reported that:

> '... from mathematics, English, social studies and science, the message is clearly emerging that images assist student learning by providing clearer meanings for concepts they must learn... Images are not only used to build understanding of singular concepts but also are used to make connections between sets of knowledge and between the science disciplines themselves' (2011:80).

Further analysis of reported studies of visual communication across the curriculum can be found in Danos (2012).

4. Categories and elements of graphicacy: key incoming and outgoing skills

Many academics' have published research concerning aspects of communication; either as an aspect of learning and/or part of the application of what has been learnt. Balchin in 1996 used the terms 'incoming' or 'outgoing' to describe these, 'according to the direction of the flow (of the information)'; different terms have been used to describe these such as reading, comprehending and drawing, as well as encoding and decoding information in graphic form (Fry, 1974:388; Molyneux & Tolley, 1987; Catling, 1995).

An important part of my research was a literature search which revealed substantial areas of agreement between the pioneer advocates of graphicacy and visual learning. Although they did not use the same terminology, it proved possible to group their findings together in a coherent way. Tables 1 and 2 below summarize the information gathered through literature, regarding graphicacy categories and elements, and key related incoming and outgoing skills. The key authors from which the ideas were drawn included: Archer (1973), Balchin (1985), Liben & Downs, (1993), Anning (1997), Poracsky et al. (1999), Wilmot (1999), Adams & Baynes (2001), van Harmelen (2002), Riding & Boardman (1983), Roth et al (2005), Åberg-Bengtsson (2006) and Cross (2006). Where applicable, the author(s) from whom ideas or terms have been taken are noted. For example, the term Art has been used in the context defined by Archer in 1973, and its definition is matched with those closely related from other findings in literature. The tables were created both to summarize the results of the literature review and to enable patterns to emerge, including consistent and conflicting views in regards to image use, skills and knowledge required to read and interpret or create them etc.

Often authors talked about a group of images requiring a set of skills to create or understand them. For that reason, when images are broken down into categories, some repetition occurs. Table 1 shows the seven categories of graphicacy images that emerged, and some of the elements of which they were comprised, namely:

- Artistic;
- Drawing;
- Diagrammatic;
- CAD;
- Sequential;
- Symbolic;
- Omitted.

Omitted is a category created by Fry, for the images which incorporate miscellaneous graphicacy elements, different from those identified in the other categories, and consequently, in which they could not be placed.

Table 2 shows the key skills and abilities which were identified as being required to deal with each of these categories. They have been grouped according to the direction of flow of information; incoming and outgoing perspectives, which were the terms given by Balchin (1976) relating to understanding and creating of images:

- The artistic category can be distinguished from drawings, as the latter have been identified to be accurate representations of thoughts, ideas or scenes.
- Images in the diagrams category convey some kind of technical information.
- CAD images are created using computer software and the outgoing skills appear to outnumber the incoming skills, in regards to the potential depth of complexity offered by the handling of each software and tools to be used.
- The elements in the sequential category require a logical flow when illustrating information. This is another category which seems easier to understand and learn from an incoming perspective when compared with the outgoing skills required.
- The symbolic category includes both Fry's (1981) quantitative and spatial categories and other elements; maps/cartograms, photographs and posters/advertisements, which represent a message, a person, a scene or an area. Symbols were referred to by a number of authors regarding the skills required to deal with them.

Both incoming and outgoing skills related to graphicacy categories provide clear links between elements of graphicacy and external activities, many of which are closely related to designing. This is well-recognized in general terms, but detailed research of the relationships between graphicacy and design education has yet to be conducted in sufficient depth in order to establish causal relationships.

TABLE 1 GRAPHICACY CATEGORIES AND ELEMENTS (Danos, 2014: 62)

Image categories	Elements	References
ARTISTIC [referred to by Fry (1981) as *Pictorial* and by Balchin (1985) as *Graphic arts*]	Art	Archer, 1973
	Life drawing	Anning, 1997
	Landscape drawing	Balchin, 1985; Anning, 1997; Adams & Baynes, 2001
	Portraits	Anning, 1997
	Still life	Anning, 1997; Adams & Baynes, 2001
DRAWING [referred to by Fry (1981) as *Pictorial*]	Drafts	Anning, 1997
	Sketching	Anning, 1997; Wilmot, 1999; Adams & Baynes, 2001
	Drawing	Anning, 1997; Adams & Baynes, 2001
DIAGRAMMATIC [referred to by Fry(1981), Balchin (1985), Anning (1997), Wilmot (1999) and Adams & Baynes (2001), as *Pictorial*]	Annotated	Anning, 1997; Adams & Baynes, 2001
	Engineering/technical	Riding & Boardman, 1983; Anning, 1997; Adams & Baynes, 2001
	Architectural	Balchin, 1985; Anning, 1997
	Projections (Orthographic, oblique, isometric)	Anning, 1997; Adams & Baynes, 2001
	Perspective	Norman (private conversation, 2008)
	Exploded	Anning, 1997; Adams & Baynes, 2001
CAD [referred to by Balchin (1996) as *Computer Graphics*]	3D virtual environment	Balchin, 1985; Anning, 1997; Adams & Baynes, 2001
	3D virtual products	Balchin, 1985; Anning, 1997; Adams & Baynes, 2001
SEQUENTIAL [referred to by Fry (1981) as *Lineal*]	Cartoons	Anning, 1997; Wilmot, 1999; Adams & Baynes, 2001
	Story boards	Anning, 1997; Adams & Baynes, 2001
SYMBOLIC [referred to by Fry (1981) as *Quantitative* or *Spatial*, and by Anning (1997) as *Mathematical*]	Charts	Balchin, 1985 ; Åberg-Bengtsson & Ottosson, 2006; Anning, 1997
	Graphs	Riding & Boardman, 1983; Balchin, 1985; Wilmot, 1999; Roth, 2005; Åberg-Bengtsson & Ottosson, 2006
	Maps/cartograms	Riding & Boardman, 1983; Balchin, 1985 and 1996; Wilmot, 1999; Adams & Baynes, 2001; Åberg-Bengtsson & Ottosson, 2006
	Photographs	Boardman, 1976; Balchin, 1985 and 1996; Wilmot, 1999; Roth, 2005
	Posters/advertisements	Wilmot, 1999
OMITTED [referred to by Fry, 1981]	Symbols	Balchin, 1985; Anning, 1997

TABLE 2 KEY INCOMING AND OUTGOING SKILLS (Danos, 2014: 63-64)

Image categories	Incoming skills	Outgoing skills
ARTISTIC	• Perception, sensibility and handling of emotional meaning *(Archer, 1973)* • Artistic statement *(Anning, 1997)* • Communicate sensory and emotional data *(Poracsky et al., 1999)* • Analogy, metaphors, evaluation, imagination, subjectivity *(Cross, 2006)*	• Learn to see and feel what you see, eye-hand coordination, translating a perceived image into a graphic outcome *(Anning, 1997)* • Perception; observe, record, investigate, examine, experiment, analyse, synthesize, contemplate, remember, reflect, respond emotionally *(Adams & Baynes, 2001)*
DRAWING	• Envision artefacts, formulate or record plans, rehearse, clarify and explore ideas or feelings *(Anning, 1997)* • Convey spatial information, utilize some form of symbolic language *(Wilmot, 1999)* • Reflection, critical thinking *(Cross, 2006)*	• Learn to see and feel what you see, eye-hand coordination, translating a perceived image into a graphic outcome *(Anning, 1997)* • Convey spatial information, utilize some form of symbolic language *(Wilmot, 1999)* • Perception; observe, record, investigate, examine, experiment, analyse, synthesize, contemplate, remember, reflect, respond emotionally. Manipulate; imagine, fantasize, visualize, hypothesize, test an idea, transform, plan, solve a problem. Communication; symbolize, narrate, illustrate, interpret, explain, negotiate, instruct, specify, codify, document, record, develop *(Adams & Baynes, 2001)*
DIAGRAMMATIC	• Special-visual ability. Discriminate various symbols, analyse their meaning and relation to adjacent symbols. Construct an internal representation of the information *(Boardman, 1983)* • Communicate or converse *(Anning, 1997)* • Conceptualization, integrative thinking *(Poracsky et al., 1999)* • Decode information in graphic forms *(Wilmot, 1999)* • Spatial development *(van Harmelen, 2002)* • Objectivity, rationality, neutrality *(Cross, 2006)* • Practicality, ingenuity, empathy, concern for appropriateness *(Cross, 2006)*	• Convey spatial information, utilize some form of symbolic language, encode information in graphic forms *(Wilmot, 1999)* • Communication; symbolize, narrate, illustrate, interpret, explain, negotiate, instruct, specify, codify, document, record, develop. Manipulate; imagine, fantasize, visualize, hypothesize, test an idea, transform, plan, solve a problem *(Adams & Baynes, 2001)* • Spatial development *(van Harmelen, 2002)*

AD	• Communicate or converse *(Anning, 1997)* • Conceptualization, integrative thinking *(Poracsky et al., 1999)*	• Perception; observe, record, investigate, examine, experiment, analyse, synthesize, contemplate, remember, reflect, respond emotionally. Manipulate; imagine, fantasize, visualize, hypothesize, test an idea, transform, plan, solve a problem. Communication; symbolize, narrate, illustrate, interpret, explain, negotiate, instruct, specify, codify, document, record, develop *(Adams & Baynes 2001)*
QUENTIAL	• Communicate or converse, formulate and record plans *(Anning, 1997)* • Spatial development *(van Harmelen, 2002)*	• Convey spatial information, utilize some form of symbolic language *(Wilmot, 1999)* • Manipulate; imagine, fantasize, visualize, hypothesize, test an idea, transform, plan, solve a problem. Communication; symbolize, narrate, illustrate, interpret, explain, negotiate, instruct, specify, codify, document, record, develop *(Adams & Baynes 2001)* • Spatial development *(van Harmelen, 2002)*
MBOLIC	• Pattern recognition *(Balchin, 1976)* • Communicate spatial information, uses a complicated artificial language to convey information about selected aspects of the natural and cultural environment *(Boardman, 1976)* • Spatial-visual ability. Discriminate various symbols, analyse their meaning and relation to adjacent symbols. Construct an internal representation of the information *(Boardman, 1983)* • Understanding representational and geometric correspondences, spatial cognition *(Liben & Downs, 1993)* • Communicate or converse *(Anning, 1997)* • Communicate relative values, qualitative graphics and quantitative comparisons, numerical trends, capture connection, conceptualization *(Poracsky et al., 1999)* • Encode information in graphic forms *(Wilmot, 1999)* • Spatial development *(van Harmelen, 2002)* • Handle and communicate quantitative information. Record, analyse and communicate data. Rely on visual or spatial abilities. Ability to locate specific information, perception of trends and patterns, and the extraction of global information *(Åberg-Bengtsson, 2006)* • Objectivity, rationality, neutrality *(Cross, 2006)*	• Pattern recognition *(Balchin, 1976)* • Spatial concepts and perceptual ability *(Boardman, 1976)* • Convey spatial information, utilize some form of symbolic language *(Wilmot, 1999)* • Perception; observe, record, investigate, examine, experiment, analyse, synthesize, contemplate, remember, reflect, respond emotionally. Manipulate; imagine, fantasize, visualize, hypothesize, test an idea, transform, plan, solve a problem. Communication; symbolize, narrate, illustrate, interpret, explain, negotiate, instruct, specify, codify, document, record, develop *(Adams & Baynes 2001)* • Spatial development *(van Harmelen, 2002)*
MITTED	• Communicate or converse, formulate and record plans *(Anning, 1997)* • Objectivity, rationality, neutrality *(Cross, 2006)*	• Perception; observe, record, investigate, examine, experiment, analyse, synthesize, contemplate, remember, reflect, respond emotionally *(Adams & Baynes 2001)*

5. A taxonomy of graphicacy

Fry's taxonomy was the closest one identified relating to a research tool for studying graphicacy within the curricula. He published a wide-ranging taxonomy categorizing images according to the type of information represented, i.e., quantitative, spatial, lineal, etc. He illustrated these categories with examples probably drawn from the images most commonly used in education at the time, which are not representative of the examples used today. As times have moved on, the Internet has emerged, and computer drawing tools have become more common in schools, and the nature of drawing within the school curriculum provision has changed with the additional use of colour, photographic, and 3D images, to name a few. Hence, Fry's taxonomy needed an update and a 'make-over'.

The new taxonomy has to serve as a research tool to map graphicacy across the curriculum, and ultimately to support the identification of the skills and abilities to communicate through still visual images. To achieve these goals, the categories have to be organized so as to accommodate all types of images, grouped according to the different types of understanding one requires to be able to create or read and understand these. For example, symbolic representations such as maps and symbols use colours, shapes and lines and other elements to represent ideas and allow comparisons between features to be made. This new taxonomy shown in Figure 4.13 is a modern, cross-curricular framework which can be used to explore graphicacy across all years of secondary education.

Category description

PICTORIAL; WESTERN ART

LIFE DRAWING   LANDSCAPE   STILL LIFE   PORTRAITS   OTHER COMPOSITIONS

- Representations from an individual artistic perspective.
- Usually the item produced is a finished product itself.
- To be decoded, the observer needs to interpret these images within the artists' cultural, educational or professional context.

PICTORIAL; DRAWING

DRAFTS   SKETCHING   DRAWING

- Products finished to an appropriate level of accuracy to closely mirror an idea/observation.
- This is often a means to achieve/ get to the next stage.
- To be decoded the observer needs to identify the idea/observation.

PICTORIAL; DIAGRAMS

PERSPECTIVE   ARCHITECTURAL   ENGINEERING / TECHNICAL   EXPLODED   PROJECTIONS

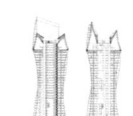
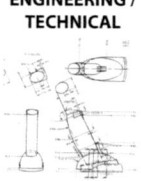
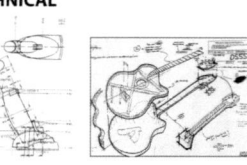

- Technical diagrams to define clearly features, details and/or requirements such as relationships, processes, components.
- To be decoded, the observer has to have developed the relevant spatial abilities and understanding of the technique.

SEQUENTIAL

STORY BOARDS   **FLOW DIAGRAM**   **SPIDER DIAGRAM /**

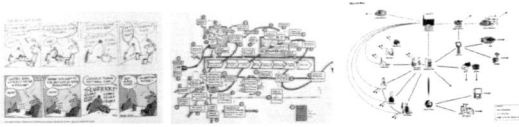

- Images which illustrate the sequence of a thought, process or story.
- Information follows a relative sense of direction.
- To be decoded, the observer needs to be able to identify the flow of information.

SYMBOLIC; QUANTITATIVE/ ABSTRACT

CHARTS & GRAPHS   **SYMBOLS**

- Symbolic representation of data, information and/or warnings.
- To be decoded the observer must recognise and make connections between the data and/or information represented.

SYMBOLIC; SPATIAL

MAPS   **ADVERTISEMENTS**

- Representations of a message, a person, a scene or an area.
- To be decoded the observer must recognise and make connections between the messages represented.

PHOTOGRAPHIC

PHOTOGRAPHS

- Relating to photographs, especially representing or simulating something with great accuracy and fidelity of detail.
- To be decoded the requirements might include any of the above, but the capabilities required to create them depends on the hardware and software used.

CAD (Computer Aided Design)

COMPUTER AIDED IMAGES   **3D VIRTUAL IMAGES**

- 2 Dimensional and 3 Dimensional images created with the use of computer software.
- To be decoded the requirements might include any of the above, but the capabilities required to create them depends on the software package.

OTHER

Games, Crosswords, Puzzles etc.

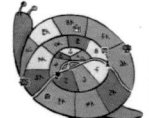 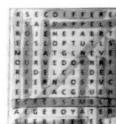 

- Other miscellaneous still visual images.

Figure 4.13 A taxonomy of graphicacy (Danos, 2014: 153)

Using the taxonomy of graphicacy

The taxonomy went through thorough analysis and review to be shaped and validated, and is considered to be work-in-progress. It has so far been:

- Published in a book (Danos, 2014) and in scientific journals; (Danos et, al. 2014; Danos & Norman, 2009, 2011, 2013);
- Presented and reviewed at conferences such as:

    - ASEE Engineering Design Graphics Division, 67th Mid-Year Conference, *Universal Graphics Multiple Perspectives*, University of Limerick, November 2012
    - International Design and Technology Educational Research (IDATER online) Conference, *Graphicacy and Modelling Conference*, University of Limerick, Ireland, December 2010
    - Cyprus Ministry of Education and Culture, *A Technological Dimension of General Education as a Necessary Element,* October 2010

- Printed in *Designing* (UK) National Education Magazine in 2009;
- Successfully used by other users during a co-research study with research students at Sheffield Hallam University;
- Placed under scrutiny during a Delphi study with experts in the field within Europe (Danos, 2012; Danos & Norman, 2013);
- Successfully used to map and identify the use of images in textbooks across the curriculum in three countries, Cyprus, UK and USA (Danos & Norman, 2011 & 2012; Danos, 2012);
- Successfully used to map and identify all images used by a range of professionals from all walks of life, as was presented by the *Quick on the Draw* exhibition, by Ken Baynes, including artists, a theatre designer, window cleaner and rally car racing driver;
- Successfully used to map and identify the use of images as used by professionals in their everyday working lives, such as a biologist, a doctor and a dentist through case studies (Danos, 2014).

6. Developmental stages

An effort to collate what we do know about the development of graphicacy has been completed and presented briefly below. Some of the well-established work that does exist, derived from literature, show a synthesis of work related to developmental stages of graphicacy skills by Kellogg, Gaitskell and Lowenfeld and demonstrate that humans have some potential to develop graphicacy up to a certain level, naturally. Three main authors' work is most commonly referenced to in structuring the review as summarized in Figure 4.14. Each author's work is from a different perspective, all very well established within many educational contexts. Kellogg was a teacher and an academic. Her findings are based on years of research and the study of thousands of images. Lowenfeld was studying intellectual and psychological growth and development and how that relates or is reflected through children's drawings. Gaitskell worked closely with school teachers, and the aim of his research was to provide guidelines for teaching and evaluating students' art.

Understanding the differences between incoming and outgoing skills related to graphicacy and linking these to external activities could support the emergence of understanding of graphicacy's role in human development and in our capability to design. Such work could reinforce and develop the work completed by Kellogg, Gaitskell and Lowenfeld. The taxonomy of graphicacy developed demonstrates that it is possible to break down this challenge systematically and link graphicacy skills and design activities in particular categories.

The development of graphicacy skills appears to be rapid, as clear progression has been noted within approximately every 6 months, starting from infant stage to around 8 to 9 years of age. Detailed work has been conducted by Kellogg in the 1970s, which describes the stages children go through in drawing, from ages 1 ½ to 8 years old. Other academics and scientists have looked at this in a more generic way, identifying stages covering longer periods of development time (2 years and more). Academics, scientists and other authors have described stages children go through during the years from 11-14 covering different aspects of development, but the information found has been rather vague. Detailed work focused on that age range (11-14 years old) could be very beneficial to both educators and the research culture.

Figure 4.14 Kellogg, Gaitskell and Lowenfeld's developmental stages (Danos, 2014: 88)

7. Teaching and learning

During my work for the PhD (Danos, 2012) I conducted a number of case studies designed to show that graphicacy could be nurtured by structured teaching and learning. It was considered essential to show that graphicacy could in fact be effectively taught. Here is an example of the kind of activity involved: a case study involving two different groups of participants; one with students aged 11-12 and another with adults aged 20-27, focusing on portrait drawings (Figure 4.15). During the case study, a workshop was organized with various practical tasks, designed to allow the participants to illustrate their capabilities in the beginning and at the end of the workshop. In between, tasks were designed to allow for the graduate development of their graphicacy skills in relation to portrait drawings, by merging drawing tips and techniques, with building an understanding of the shapes, dimensions and positioning of the key elements for the creation of a generic portrait. With the group of adults, the workshop continued further by introducing further observational and drawing skills, requesting them to create a self-portrait, based on the generic profile they had learn how to create. The results in both groups, showed a substantial difference between the task completed with no help (Task A) before the lesson and the task completed after the lesson (Task E).

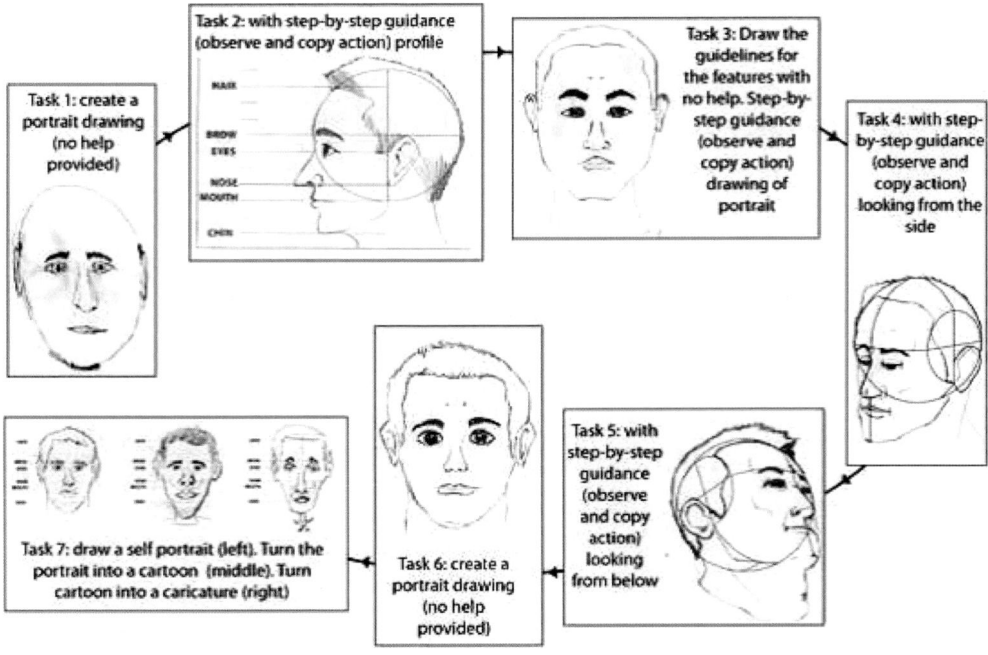

Figure 4.15 The sequence of tasks for the portrait drawing case studies. Tasks 4 and 5 were only completed with the group of adults (Danos, 2014: 99)

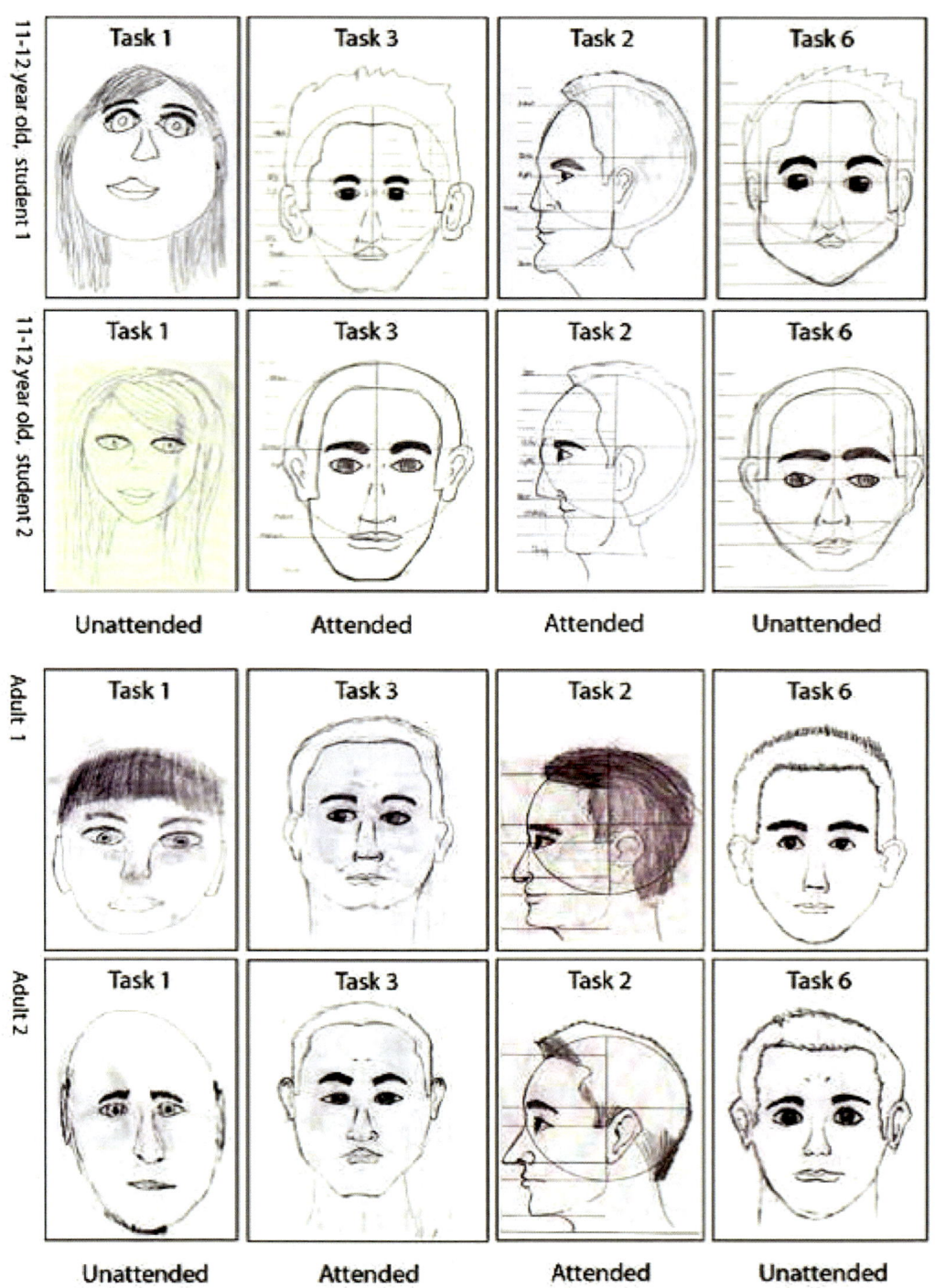

Figure 4.16 Evidence of nature and nurture (a) Year 7 students' work (11-12 years old) (b) Adults 'work (aged 22+)(Danos, 2014: 100)

The evidence for the potential of nurture to enhance graphicacy capabilities is clearly visible through comparison of the two unattended drawing tasks illustrated in Figure 4.16 (Tasks 1 and 6). During the lesson (attended tasks), the quality of the drawings reached much higher levels than those attained on the first drawing. From being schematic, the drawings became pictorial and naturalistic representations.

8. Conclusion

The role of graphicacy in society is well documented and proven, making its importance for education irrefutable. This case is well documented and has been presented by academics for more than 50 years. However it has yet to be acknowledged or accepted by our culture. Our educational system is a well-oiled steam machine, in an era driven by algorithms striving to stimulate the emotions.

The fast paced technological advances will soon leave no further room for such a discordant mismatch to exist between education (within schools), the needs for successful members of our society, and the cognitive and technical skills developed in youth.

Clearly the areas of graphicacy and its relevant skills, competencies, their developmental stages, teaching and learning methodologies and tools; comprise only some of the new areas needing urgent research and understanding.

References

Åberg-Bengtsson L (2006)"Then you can take half ... almost" – elementary students learning bar graphs and pie charts. In A Computer-Based Context, *Journal Of Mathematical Behavior*, 25, 116–135

Adams E & Baynes K (2001) *Power Drawing*, The Campaign For Drawing, Laceys Printers, England

Aldrich F & Sheppard L (2000) 'Graphicacy': the fourth 'R'?', *Primary Science Review*, 64, 8 – 11

Anning A (1997) 'Drawing out ideas: graphicacy and young children', *International Journal Of Technology And Design Education* 7, 219–239

Archer B (1973) *The Need For Design Education*, Royal College Of Art, Internal Memorandum

Ausburn L (1980) *Apprentices And Literacy Educational Services*, Swinburne Technical College, Victoria, Australia , 3

Balchin W & Coleman A (1965) 'Graphicacy – the fourth 'ace' in the pack', *Times Educational Supplement*

Baynes K 2008) *Quick On The Draw Exhibition*, 17 January - 29 March 2009, Harley Gallery Welbeck, Worksop, Nottinghamshire

Baynes K (2013) *Design: Models of Change: the impact of designerly thinking on people's lives and the environment*, Loughborough Design Press, Shepshed

Baynes K & Norman E (2012), 'Modelling and designerly thinking: STEM to STEAM', *Thinking Through Drawing*, Wimbledon College of Art, 12-14 September 2012

Catling S (1995) 'Mapping the environment with children'. In De Villiers, M. (Ed.), *Developments In Primary Geography: Theory And Practice,* The Geographical Association, Graves, Sheffield, 11-18

Cross N (2006) *Designerly Ways Of Knowing*, Springer-Verlag Ltd, London

Danos X (2012) *Graphicacy Within the Secondary School Curriculum, an exploration of continuity and progression of graphicacy in children aged 11 to 15*, PhD Thesis, Loughborough University, Loughborough Design School, UK. https://dspace.lboro.ac.uk/dspace-jspui/handle/2134/9652

Danos X (2014) *Graphicacy and Culture: Refocusing on visual learning*, Loughborough Design Press Ltd, Shepshed, Leicestershire

Danos X (2014), *Graphicacy and Culture: Refocusing on Visual learning*, Loughborough Design Press Ltd, Shepshed, Leicestershire. Video available at http://www.ldpress.co.uk

Danos X, Barr R, Górska R, & Norman E (2014) 'Curriculum planning for the development of graphicacy capability: three case studies from Europe and the USA', *European Journal of Engineering Education, 39*(6), 666-684

Danos X, (2009) 'Graphicacy in the curriculum', *Designing: The Design and Technology Magazine for Schools, Colleges and Universities,* Number 84, Autumn

Danos X and Norman E W L (2009) 'The development of a new taxonomy for graphicacy'. In *D&T - A Platform for Success: The Design and Technology Association Education and International Research Conference*, Dr Eddie Norman and Dr David Spendlove (eds), The Design and Technology Association, Loughborough University, July, 69-84

Danos X and Norman E W L (2011) 'Graphicacy and students' learning', *Selected Readings of the International Visual Literacy Association: Visual Literacy in the 21st Century: Trends, Demands, and Capacities*, Maria Avgerinou et al (eds), The International Visual Literacy Association, 59-68

Danos X., & Norman E. (2012), 'Curriculum planning for the development of graphicacy', *Engineering Design Graphics Journal (EDGJ),* 76(3),13-18, http://www.edgj.org

Danos X and Norman E W L (2013) 'The validation of a research tool for the analysis of graphicacy across the curriculum and its potential for collaborative use', *Selected Readings of the International Visual Literacy Association,* The International Visual Literacy Association

Davis J F (1992) 'Power of images: creating the myths of our time, impact of images: life and culture in the media age', *Media & Values,* Issue 57, http://www.medialit.org/reading-room/power-images-creating-myths-our-time#bio

Finson K and Pederson J (2011) What are visual data and what utility do they have in science education? *Journal Of Visual Literacy*, 30(1), 66-85

Fry E (1974) 'Graphical literacy', cited in *Journal Of Reading*, 1981, 24 (5), 383-390

Fry E (1981) 'Graphical literacy', *Journal Of Reading*, 1981, 24 (5), 383-390

Gaitskell D (1951) *Children and Their Pictures*, Ryerson Press

Jones S, Tanner H & Treadaway M (2000) 'Raising standards in mathematics through effective classroom practice', *Teaching Mathematics And Its Applications*, 19(3), 125-134

Kellogg R (1959) *What Children Scribble And Why,* Palo Alto, California

Kellogg R (1967) *Child Art Collection,* Washington, DC., Microcard Editions

Kellogg R (1970) *Analyzing Children's Art,* Palo Alto, CA: Mayfield Publishing Company

Kellogg R (1979.)*Children's Drawings, Children's Mind*, New York, Avon

Kellogg R & O'Dell S (1967) *The Psychology Of Children's Art,* Del Mar, California

Krane H & Dyson L (1981) *Graphics Communication*, Education Department Victoria

Enoch L (2016) 'The power of the image', *The Guardian* https://www.theguardian.com/info/2016/jan/14/the-power-of-the-image

Hope G (2008) *Thinking And Learning Through Drawing In Primary Classrooms*, Sage, London

Liben L & Downs R (1993) 'Understanding person-space-map relations: cartographic and developmental perspectives', *Developmental Psychology*, 29(4), 739-752.

Lowenfeld V (1952) *The Nature Of Creative Activity: Experimental And Comparative Studies Of Visual And Non-Visual Sources Of Drawing, Painting And Sculpture By Means Of The Artistic Products Of Weak Sighted And Blind Subjects And The Arts Of Different Epochs And Cultures*, Routledge And Kegan Paul, London

Lowenfeld V (1954) *Your Child And His Art: A Guide For Parents,* Macmillan, New York

Lowenfeld V (1963) *Your Child And His Art, New York*, Macmillan Publishing Company

Lowenfeld V (1964) *Creative And Mental Growth, 4th Edition,* Macmillan Publishing Company, New York

Moyneux F & Tolley H (1987) *Teaching Geography,* Macmillan, London

Ochaya W (2005) *Using 3D Graphic And Animation Software To Enhance Learning Experience In GED Math,* A Capstone Project Of The Requirements For The Degree Of Master Of Science In Multidisciplinary Studies With Concentration In Information Technology, Rochester Institute Of Technology, NY

Petterson R (1993) *Visual Information,* Educational Technology Publications, Englewood Cliffs, NJ

Pinker S (1985) 'Visual Cognition: An Introduction'. In S. Pinker (Ed.), *Visual Cognition,* MIT Press, Cambridge, MA

Poracsky J, Young E P & Judy P (1999) 'The emergence of graphicacy', *The Journal Of General Education,* 48(2), 103-110

Riding R & Boardman D (1983) 'The relationship between sex and learning style and graphicacy in 14-year-old children', *Educational Review,* 35 (1), 69-79

Roth M (1999) 'The evolution of umwelt and communication', *Cybernetics And Human Knowing,* 6(4), 5–23

Roth M (2001) 'Gestures: their role in teaching and learning', *Review of Educational Research,* 71, 365–392.

Roth M., Ardengi P, & Han Y (2005) 'Critical graphicacy', *Understanding Visual Representation-Practices In Schools Science*

Roth M & Mcginn K (1998) 'Inscriptions: toward a theory of representing as social practice', *Review of Educational Research,* 68, 35–59.

van Harmelen U (2002) *Lego, The Missing Link In The Spatial Conceptual Chain? Investigating Graphicacy In The Southern African Context.* Unpublished Paper, Education Department, Rhodes University, Grahamstown

Verdi P, Kulhavy W, Stock A, Rittschof A, & Johnson T (1996) 'Text learning using scientific diagrams: implications for classroom use', *Contemporary Educational Psychology,* 21, 487-499

Wilmot D (1999) 'Graphicacy as a form of communication', *South African Geographical Journal* (Special Issue June) 81 (2), 91-95

5. DESIGN EPISTEMOLOGY: A WIDER PERSPECTIVE?
Ken Baynes

The current educational debate about design epistemology is partly driven by the desire to see design become an integral part of general education. A laudable aim in itself but curriculum politics is likely to lead to special pleading and lack of critical thinking. The argument from the needs of industry, engineering and the creative industries (though valid) is potentially dangerous. A better argument for inclusion in general education is that design ability is a fundamental attribute of all human beings and that fostering it will lead to desirable personal and social outcomes.

Can such an argument be made?

I believe it can. The aim of this contribution is to locate design activity in a wider historical and evolutionary context. What I want to demonstrate is that design straddles the worlds of physical reality and cultural structures. This is how design enters individual lives and provides a vehicle for social interaction. It is through material culture that the designer's imagination becomes manifest.

Design activity is not solely the province of specialists. It is also a necessity for 'ordinary' people. From the beginning they had perforce to plan ahead and create a supportive environment. It was a matter of design or die. In the main the necessary skills were learnt by growing up in an environment where they were practiced and where there was a powerful incentive both to learn and to show others how to do it.

I take it as proven that design is possible only because the human mind can make models of possible future realities. These can be shared with others through externalized models. But it is wrong to say that modelling is unique to design. Neuroscience shows us that in fact all mental processes are based on modelling. It is the mind's job to create usable models of the world from incoming sense data and then to take action as necessary. It is the particular purpose of design that determines the nature of the modelling tools used by designers.

Time
In 1981 Phil Roberts (Archer et al, 2005) suggested that it might not be particularly revealing to ask 'what is design' – a more useful question could be 'when is design'. Very little seems to have been done to follow up on this insight but it looks more and more promising as a key to design epistemology.

Since designing is essentially about changing an existing situation, time is of the essence.

Roberts was pushing away from the idea of design activity as problem solving. Instead design activity emerges in response to 'a state of affairs, in which we feel some unease or discrepancy or incompatibility'. The aim of design is to resolve this mis-match. But any such resolution is only a temporary resting place in 'a continuing series of overlapping problem states some of which may in fact develop directly, and even as a result of, the resolution of a previous problem state'.

This leads to the understanding that all design activity not only results in change but takes place in a context of change – change in the specific circumstances that led to the design and change in the surrounding designs and situations. We could visualize this as a network of interacting people, things and environments functioning in an atmosphere of beliefs, technological know-how and socio-economic competition. It might resemble a neural network. Such an analogy could prove useful as a model of how the human mind conceives of and brings about change.

The capacities of the human mind have been shaped by evolution, history and learning. The journey from hunter gatherers through the agricultural, scientific, industrial and digital revolutions may or may not be described as 'progress' and may or may not have been marked by an increase in human happiness. Indisputably, however, they have been marked by humans moving further and further away from the natural environment towards a human-made world. They have also been marked by a dramatic increase in the speed and scope of change and innovation. Yet our understanding of the dynamics of change remains rudimentary. Designers need to work with sociologists, economists and scientists to develop more reliable ways of modelling change.

BENEFIT – COST = VALUE

David Pye's *The Nature of Design* (1964) is a half-forgotten classic on the theory of design. Pye ranks – in my opinion – with Bruce Archer, Christopher Jones and Nigel Cross as a pioneer. He had the advantage of being a practicing maker (a brilliant woodworker) which gave him a keen understanding of the intractability of material. Pye's view was that the idea of function had diverted attention from all the other factors that 'limit the shape of designed things independently of the designer's preference'. He claimed that 'economy, not physics, is always the predominant influence because directly and indirectly it sets out the most limits'.

By 'economy', Pye understood something much more than money or funding. He was referring to the input of energy, ideas, material and social upheaval that go with any innovation:

'Any change originated by man (sic) exacts a cost from him. The cost is reckoned in effort, trouble, time, often in running the risk of enduring discomfort also. Adam found this out.

Economy ... must be understood as referring primarily to this unpleasant catalogue and only secondarily to the money we pay to avoid enduring it; for when we pay a price in money for a device, as a rule we are paying directly or indirectly to escape the natural cost in effort or discomfort, trouble, time or risk, of the result which the device gives.'

It is cost in this broad sense that largely determines the form of a particular design. In typically downbeat style, Pye explains that this means that every design is a compromise and so, to some degree a failure. Where you decide to compromise will shape the outcome. Although a compromise may be a brilliantly creative resolution, giving more output for less input, in no case can it be the best possible or most 'logical' outcome because 'the requirements being in conflict, their logical outcome is an impossibility ...'

Ultimately it simply depends on your priorities. Beliefs about competing values are often the basis of design decisions.

It also depends on your ability to understand the implications of your priorities. Cost benefit analysis is an attempt to provide a method for doing the kind of sum which will reveal the balance between benefit, cost and value. But it is notoriously difficult to estimate costs in advance and the technique depends for success on allocating a monetary value to every cost and every benefit. Some benefits and some costs are likely to simply vanish or not be considered relevant. The most dramatic contemporary example of unattributed costs is provided by the polluting effects of intensive agriculture. The damage done to soil, water, wild-life and the atmosphere are not reflected in the cost of food. They apparently vanish but of course will reappear one day long after the polluters have gone on their way.

There are also examples of uncosted benefits. All over Britain parks are under threat because they represent a drain on the budgets of local authorities and taxpayers. However, their value is not in dispute. They clearly help ameliorate a large range of social problems – obesity, child care, depression and loneliness to name only a few. If parks did not exist, they would create costs elsewhere in the system but it is remarkably difficult to quantify the savings that could reasonably be attributed to parks. Even more difficult is to give some kind of weight to the pleasure which parks give to millions of people.

I argue that today attempts to quantify the value that results from design activity inevitably reflects the power relations in society as much as it does the needs of people or the environment.

Society, culture and consciousness

Susan Greenfield (2017) and her team at Oxford have been searching for that most elusive of links: what is the brain activity that results in consciousness? As she acknowledges this is an enquiry that steps out of the purely scientific into the existential, philosophical and experiential. They have managed to make a clear concordance between reported episodes of conscious experience and distinctive activities in the brain involving very large waves of electrical and biochemical activity. This could be the physical basis of consciousness but as Greenhill asks: what is consciousness? She distinguishes between 'consciousness', something shared by many animals and human babies, and 'self-consciousness' something unique to humans that emerges some time after birth.

It is self-consciousness that we experience on a daily basis. Apart from the inrush of sensory data, the defining quality of self-consciousness is memory of our own past. Our unique selves are made of memories: relationships, learning, special places, stories and images. It is implicit in memories of a changing world that the future can – in fact will – be different from the past. Design and other forward facing human activities such as politics and technology make this explicit. And the desire of each unique human to, as it were, 'make' their own lives also implies a creative relationship with the future.

Consciousness by itself would not explain humanity's remarkable effectiveness in shaping the environment and taking over the world. Self-consciousness has no meaning without a context of others. Self-awareness exists not only in personal relations with other individuals but also in a complex context of human-made entities that are not themselves conscious. One effect of these entities, for example, schools, is to provide a setting in which individual minds can interact. Schools and other social institutions make it possible for individuals to contribute creatively to society and for society to nurture individuals. This is a dynamic interaction that in the right circumstances can lead to dramatic change.

In *Wired for Culture*, Mark Pagel (2012) traces the origins of the social mind. He sees the 'invention' of culture as the first decisive step away from evolution as the only engine of change. Pagel follows Richard Dawkins and Daniel Dennett in speaking of 'memes' as a kind of mental counterpart to genes. Memes express themselves in the mind and in culture: memes, like genes, compete to replicate. But Pagel resists the idea that such a single-minded struggle for survival is negative, favouring only 'a nasty and ruthless nature'. He writes:

> 'In fact, if the history of biological evolution teaches us anything, it is that natural selection can often achieve the most for its genes by building cooperation among actors or even among genes that avoid debilitating conflict, returning greater gains than could be achieved by competition or a solitary existence.'

He goes on to quote William Hamilton (writing in 1964):

'... we would expect the genetic system to have various inbuilt safeguards and to provide not a blank sheet for individual cultural development but a sheet at least lightly scrawled with certain tentative outlines ...'

In other words, human culture – the product of evolution, memory, self-consciousness and social interaction – could not take just any form but rather a form that would be generally for the benefit and ultimately survival of Homo Sapiens. Design activity is a key element in filling in the 'tentative outlines' of cultural development.

Survival strategy

My conviction is that the main driver of design activity – and incidentally technology and the arts – has been to provide a safe 'home' for Homo Sapiens and, in particular, to allow our 'big brain' to flourish.

The big brain and the resulting phenomena of mind and culture come at a price. The brain itself uses large quantities of energy that in other animals may be devoted to soaring flight, exceptional speed, or other highly specialist abilities. But the largest penalty is the difficulty of human births and the striking immaturity of human offspring when they emerge from the womb. Birth is just the starting point for a lengthy period of development and at first the child cannot fend for itself. It is entirely dependent on its mother who, in turn is dependent on the surrounding physical and social environment – essentially, things and people.

A visitor from outer space would be struck by the fact that 'homes' are the predominating structures in human settlements. Further enquiry would show many other buildings and facilities devoted to family life and the rearing of children. One element in this must be down to the competition for genetic continuity which, in the case of aristocratic and royal families, was often made explicit in dynastic marriages. In peasant societies children were a kind of wealth, their labour being an essential input in farming and family security. More complex societies have seen children as a national resource. Fundamentalist belief systems have been determined to mould children in their own image and so ensure that their beliefs (memes?) are replicated in the future.

A 'home' need not be anything resembling a house. It is, however, a place with the equipment necessary for family life. In nomadic cultures the 'home' is portable but still consists of the utensils, clothes, blankets and tools that make survival possible. This basic kit of parts has, over the centuries, been elaborated into a support system of great complexity. Just as individual consciousness is embedded in social and personal relations, so too the home environment of a family in the industrialized world has come to rely on a global network of economic, technological and digital systems.

One criterion for success or failure in any design enterprise should be its ability to make secure individuals, families, communities and their wider support systems.

Materialization

The 'things' that support human life are complemented by beliefs and customs which are accepted and, indeed, celebrated by the members of that particular group. It is a key characteristic of human communities that material and mental environments express and reinforce each other. Thus, in a medieval city the cathedral and other religious buildings dominate a plan that reflects the pervasive Catholic ideology. In contrast, today's city of London is dominated by grand, spectacular office buildings that celebrate the power and 'truth' of capitalism.

The pre-historian Colin Renfrew (2007) discusses the significance of 'materialization' in the emergence of human culture. He argues that the engagement of early humans with things they had designed and made created a new kind of interrelationship with the material world: 'Material engagement theory considers the processes by which human individuals and communities engage with the material world through actions that have simultaneously a material reality and a cognitive or intelligent component'. He notes the significance of 'institutional facts' for human society. Institutional facts are the ideological glue which binds together the disparate members of a particular society and which enable it to grow on the basis of shared assumptions. These institutional facts are then directly embodied in the designed world since, for example, the form of a home is dictated by the prevailing beliefs and customs about family life, the relationships between men and women and ideals of child-care as well as climate, available technology and building materials.

Materialization also holds the key to the importance of aesthetics in anything made by people. Music, sculpture, books, buildings, clothes, theatre, Facebook pages – all are expressed in 'qualia'. Qualia are first the qualitative models that the human mind attributes to sensory inputs: second they are the qualitative values attributed by the mind to the products of its own imagination.

The American evolutionary biologist E O Wilson (2012) traces the origins of aesthetic perceptions to the experiences of hunter gatherers. But it seems equally likely that the experience of making things taught early craftspeople to value the intrinsic structures locked up in natural materials. Later these would be elaborated into an appreciation of form that the mind could label 'beautiful'. Beautiful places and things proved to be deeply satisfying and meaningful. In their extraordinary study of the patterns of towns, buildings and constructions, Christopher Alexander (1977) and his team at the Centre for Environmental Structure at Berkley managed to identify the aesthetic 'language' of human settlements. Their work provides a vivid example of the way in which humans have 'filled in' the tentative outlines provided by evolution.

Epistemology

Any epistemology of design will thus need to accommodate four key points:

1. The intention of design activity is to support the survival of Homo Sapiens;
2. The intention of design activity is to help create a safe place for the further development of humanity's cognitive abilities;
3. Design operates in the area where the physical environment interacts with and influences the cultural/mental environment of 'institutional facts';
4. Design is determined by technology, social and personal beliefs and aesthetic perceptions.

In other words, the interaction of material and ideological worlds.

These statements at a very high level of generalization. Far too high to be of practical use at a more everyday level. However, they could be used as the starting points for a series of more specific questions which could provide a usable framework for considering design, the results of design and design education.

WHAT IS THE INTENTION OF DESIGN ACTIVITY?
HOW IS THE INTENTION OF DESIGN ACTIVITY REALIZED?
WHAT KNOWLEDGE AND VALUES ARE USED IN DESIGN ACTIVITY?
HOW RELIABLE ARE THE METHODS USED IN DESIGN ACTIVITY?
HOW IS THE BENEFIT OF DESIGN ACTIVITY EVALUATED?
HOW IS THE KNOWLEDGE GAINED BY DESIGN ACTIVITY RECORDED, EVALUATED AND PASSED ON?

These questions too are at a high level of generality. However, they can be made specific. For example:

What is the intention of design activity?

Can become:

What is the intention of THIS design activity?

And so on, down the questions.
Equally, they could become more focused on research, teaching or what Brochocka and Roberts (Archer et al, 2005) call 'the transitive mode' – the designerly activity undertaken by the user or consumer:

What is the intention of THIS programme of design RESEARCH?
What is the intention of THIS curriculum of design EDUCATIONAL activity?
What is the intention of THIS specification for the design of a HOSPITAL BED?
What is the intention of MY purchase of THIS design?

The interaction of material and ideological worlds has been dynamic and has become more dynamic and far reaching over time. The Israeli historian, Yuval Noah Harari (2011) describes institutional facts as 'myths or stories', meaning that they have meaning only for humans. But this does not mean that they are trivial or that they are lies. He writes:

'The kinds of things that people create through this network of stories are known in academic circles as 'fictions', 'social constructs' or 'imagined realities'...

'Unlike lying, an imagined reality is something that everyone believes in, and as long as this communal belief persists, the imagined reality exerts force in the world ...

'Ever since the Cognitive Revolution, Sapiens have thus been living in a dual reality. On the one hand, the objective reality of rivers, trees and lions; and on the other hand, the imagined reality of gods, nations and corporations. As time went by, the imagined reality became ever more powerful, so that today the very survival of rivers, trees and lions depends on the grace of imagined entities such as the United States and Google.'

The imagined realities created by designers depend for their realization in objective reality on the social constructs shared by individuals and institutions.

References

Christopher Alexander, Sara Ishikawa and Murray Silverstein (1977), *A Pattern Language: Towns building construction*, Oxford University Press, New York

Bruce Archer, Ken Baynes and Phil Roberts (2005), *A Framework for Design and Design Education: a reader containing key papers from the 1970s and 1980s*, The Design and Technology Association, Wellesbourne

Susan Greenfield (2017), *A Day in the Life of the Brain: the neuroscience of consciousness from dawn to dusk*, Penguin Books, London

Yuval Noah Harari (2014), *Sapiens: a brief history of humankind*, Vintage Books, London. First published in Hebrew, 2011

Mark Pagel (2012), *Wired for Culture: origins of the human social mind*, W W Norton & Company, New York

David Pye (1964), *The Nature of Design*, Studio Vista

Colin Renfrew (2007), *Prehistory: the making of the human mind*, Weidenfeld and Nicolson, London

Edward O Wilson (2012), *The Social Conquest of Earth*, Liveright Publishing Corporation, New York

6. MAKING FURTHER PROGRESS
Eddie Norman & Ken Baynes

The passage shown below was written by the Department of Education's Expert Panel in 2011. It is hard to believe that any informed person would have given it any weight or taken it seriously. What evidence could the Expert Panel have been considering? Design education does not provide 'powerful ways of engaging with the future' ... how could such a statement ever be credible, as it would almost serve as a useful definition of design education? However this viewpoint has seemingly subsequently facilitated much damage to design education in schools.

'4.8 Despite their importance in balanced educational provision, we are not entirely persuaded of claims that design and technology, information and communication technology and citizenship have sufficient disciplinary coherence[58] to be stated as discrete and separate National Curriculum 'subjects'. We recommend that:

Design and technology is reclassified as part of the Basic Curriculum. We recommend that design and technology programmes should be developed by schools in response to local needs and interests, which is why we take the view that a reclassification to the Basic Curriculum is desirable.

...

[58] Implicit in this judgement is a view of disciplinary knowledge as a distinct way of investigating, knowing and making sense with particular foci, procedures and theories, reflecting both cumulative understanding and powerful ways of engaging with the future. In this sense, disciplinary knowledge offers core foundations for education, from which the subjects of the curriculum are derived. Some very worthwhile areas of learning apply such knowledge in particular ways or foreground particular areas of skill or competence – but have weaker epistemological roots. Our judgement about possible reclassification is based on the balance of advantage, given the need to reduce prescription in the National Curriculum.' (Department for Education, 2011:24)

The strangeness of this statement from the perspective of design education in universities can be illustrated by noting the investigation published by *Business Week* in 2010, which was approximately concurrent (Blomberg, 2010). They presented a 'snapshot of the nascent movement to teach design thinking and innovation to a new generation of global corporate leaders'. The 30 programmes they selected as the 'world's best' were presented in a slide show and are listed alphabetically below.

- Masters in Industrial Design: *Art Center College of Design*/MBA (INSEAD) ... Pasadena, California/Fontainebleau, France or Singapore
- MBA in Design Strategy: *California College of the Arts* ... San Francisco, California

- Masters in Product Development: *Carnegie Mellon University* … Pittsburgh, Pennsylvania
- MBA: *Case Western Reserve University* … Cleveland, Ohio
- Masters in Service & Product Design: *Chiba University* … Japan
- Masters in Design Management: *China Central Academy of Fine Arts* … Beijing
- Masters in Design in Innovation and Creativity in Industry: *Cranfield University/University of the Arts London*… Cranfield, UK, London
- Masters in Strategic Product Design: *Delft University of Technology* … Delft, The Netherlands
- Masters in Business Design: *Domus Academy* … Milan, Italy
- International Design Business Management: *Helsinki School of Economics/ University of Art and Design Helsinki/Helsinki University of Technology* … Helsinki, Finland
- Masters in Design (Design Strategies): *Hong Kong Polytechnic University* … Hong Kong, China
- Dual degree Master of Design and MBA: *Illinois Institute of Technology* … Chicago, Illinois
- MBA, Executive MBA, Weekend Executive MBA: *Imperial College/Design London* … London, UK
- Masters in Industrial Design: *Korea Advanced Institute of Science and Technology* … Daejeon, Korea
- Strategic Design Management post-graduate degree: *National Institute of Design* … Ahmedabad, India
- Masters in Product Development: *Northwestern University* … Evanston, Illinois
- MBA Emotional Design: *Pontifícia Universidade Católica do Paraná* … Paraná, Brazil
- Masters of Professional Studies in Design Management: *Pratt Institute* … New York
- Dual degree Innovation Design Engineering: *Royal College of Art/Imperial College* … London, UK
- Masters in Design Management: *Savannah College of Art and Design* … Savannah, Georgia
- MFA Designer As Author: *School of Visual Arts* … New York
- Masters in Industrial Design: *Shih Chien University* …Taipei, Taiwan
- Joint Program in Design and the Hasso Plattner Institute of Design (d.school): *Stanford University* … Stanford, California
- Executive MBA with concentration in Innovation & Design Management: *Suffolk University* … Boston, Massachusetts
- Masters in Industrial Design: *Umeå University* … Umeå, Sweden
- MBA: *University of California* … Berkeley, California
- Masters in Design: *University of Cincinnati* … Cincinnati, Ohio
- Masters in Business & Design: *University of Gothenburg* … Gothenburg, Sweden
- MBA: *University of Toronto* … Ontario, Canada

It is apparent that there is some kind of mismatch between 'design thinking' as perceived in higher education and the view held by the Expert Panel concerning design epistemology, but there is clearly much work to be done in articulating that mismatch. It is also important to consider whether such a mismatch was a pivotal influence on the trajectory of design and technology education. Design and technology education may already have been following a path to decline that the Expert Panel's intervention exacerbated.

The Editorial from June 2012 acknowledged that a design and technology curriculum 'derived from the lobbying conducted by special interest groups and selective curriculum development projects tends to be something of a patchwork and lacks a core disciplinary strand' (p9), but it is a long way from there to the Expert Panel's view that design education does not provide 'powerful ways of engaging with the future'. The contribution by Stephanie Atkinson (Section 3.1) presents a more complete picture of how the D&T community have collectively allowed an appearance of a lack of disciplinary coherence to develop and take hold as a view of the contribution of D&T to children's education. However, it remains remarkable that an Expert Panel charged with looking towards a curriculum fit for the 21st Century was not looking beyond past mistakes. The subsequent government decisions detailed by Stephanie Atkinson and Alison Hardy (Section 3.2) concerning Key Stage 4, the Ebacc, and new school performance measures do not suggest any weakening of these adverse perceptions, and also point towards a future of continuing marginalization for design education within school curricula.

Alison Hardy's contribution takes us to the heart of the political situation within which the Expert Panel's judgement was reached and reinforces the view that D&T's decline is essentially driven by particular epistemological positions. Clearly design departments in higher education would not recognise a theoretical position that suggested that they did not embody powerful knowledge, neither would they accept that the knowledge they embody actually belonged in a different faculty and their role was applying it. Of course, D&T in schools is a different matter in that its curriculum needs to reflect interests other than design, such as those of engineering and craft, but nevertheless it could be concluded that D&T in general education has allowed too great a gap to develop between its curriculum and design curricula in higher education so that it has become vulnerable to such criticisms. Alternatively, it might be argued that design epistemology has not been adequately articulated by academics in higher education in order to achieve general acceptance in society, and hence presented policymakers with difficulties that they were unable to resolve in the available timescales. Or, perhaps both of these positions are factors, and no doubt along with others.

From a different perspective, as presented in Steve Keirl's contribution (Section 3.3), it is possible to see the design curriculum in general curriculum as having moved too far in the direction of the curricula offered in higher education. Many design programmes in higher education tend to have vocational elements alongside the further development of the students' general design capabilities. With the introduction of fees for undergraduate courses there follows the realization that the students are investing in their education and there is an expectation of an immediate return. Of course when the undergraduate programmes were funded by the government there was still an expectation of a return to society, but that could be framed in longer term criteria. Hence design courses in higher education often focus on a particular design area for which potentially relevant knowledge, skills and values can be identified from common tasks and products (further discussion of this possibility can be found in Norman, 1998). Steve Keirl makes clear that design epistemology in general education is quite a different matter. Although design epistemology in general and higher education must have common threads, they are perhaps best approached from different directions.

The fluid nature of design knowledge is demonstrated in the contributions by both Graham Newman (Section 3.4) and Tristram Shepard (Section 3.5). Graham Newman describes the building blocks of design epistemology as 'rules, critical reflection, collaboration and research'; fundamental principles which evolve within a culture of practice. He quotes David Hitner's view that '… it's important to know the rules in order to start to break them or adapt them'. There are matters to be taught in design education, and things for students to learn before they move on to challenging apparent boundaries. In his contribution, Tristram Shepard spells out what some of those matters and things could be. It is not hard to imagine a design education curriculum constructed along the lines he suggests, but this is not the current direction of travel. As he says:

> 'The new Awarding Organization D&T specifications contain extensive and explicit coverage of a knowledge of the properties, processes and tools relating to traditional materials, while only superficially mentioning design skills and learning about people's physical and psychological needs and the interface between users and products, places and communications.' (p32)

'Design education' and 'technology' are clearly finding each other to be hard bedfellows. The perceived need to express the real constraints that are implicit in particular technologies perhaps over-powering the subtleties and complexities that need to be overcome in order to articulate design epistemology.

Tristram Shepard's contribution ends with a call for design education to find a new place in the school curriculum so that its general aims that emerged in the 1960s and 70s can be more effectively pursued. David Spendlove's (Section 3.6) contribution extends that perspective and calls for the emergence of 'Design and/or Technology 2.0'; the prevailing model 'Design and/or Technology 1.0' having reached the end of its lifespan. As he says (p.40):

> 'As such if we consider the current prevailing model of design and technology in schools to be conceived of as design and technology version 1.0 we can then

recognise version 1.0 may be coming to the end of its lifespan. Whilst we could also go into the nuances in that we might be currently operating on version 1.5 or 1.6, for now we can say that 1.0 characterizes a model of delivery that enjoyed incredible success, at times, but that given some of the circumstances outlined, is now coming to the end of its lifecycle.'

David Spendlove calls for 'Design and/or Technology 2.0' to have design thinking as its catalyst, which must surely be the way forward and also makes some of the difficulties apparent, not least the continuing difficulties in articulating its meaning. Nevertheless, as he states, and an internet search will confirm, design thinking is already gaining footholds in general education across the world.

Philosophy of technology

There is extensive literature concerning the philosophy of technology and it is not appropriate to attempt to either review or summarize it here. Interested readers might consider exploring Marc de Vries' book *Teaching About Technology: An Introduction to the Philosophy of Technology for Non-philosophers* (2005). Some selected passages are quoted here, together with something of their context, in order to give a flavour of what can be found.

Chapter 3 (de Vries, 2005) is concerned with 'Technological Knowledge'. The traditional view of knowledge is discussed as *justified true belief* and it is then explained that technological knowledge 'does not fit well with this definition' (ibid: 31) for several reasons:
- firstly, that there is some technological knowledge that cannot be expressed properly in propositions;
- secondly, that some technological knowledge is expressed in sketches and drawings;
- thirdly, that some technological knowledge is normative;
- finally, 'it can be questioned if 'truth' is the primary condition that engineers are interested in when they seek knowledge'. (ibid: 33)

So, there are difficulties. The concept of acceptances rather than beliefs is discussed as an alternative approach and taxonomies of technological knowledge explored. This section ends with a taxonomy embodying Dooyeweerd's aspects of reality, a follows:

'a) Knowledge of the physical nature (non-intentional aspects, in which the artefact can serve as a subject)
   i) The arithmetical aspects
   ii) The spatial aspects
   iii) The kinematical aspects
   iv) The physical aspects
   v) The biotic aspects

b) Knowledge of the functional nature (intentional aspects, in which the artefact can only serve as an object to which a subject ascribes a function)
  i) The sensitive aspects
  ii) The logical aspects
  iii) The historical aspects
  iv) The lingual aspects
  v) The social aspects
  vi) The economic aspects
  vii) The aesthetic aspects
  viii) The juridical aspects
  ix) The ethical aspects
  x) The pistic aspects

> This extended taxonomy offers a more detailed picture of the complexity of the knowledge that is needed to design the artefact than the division into the physical and functional aspects yields.' (ibid:37)

However, there is some way to go before the forms such knowledge can take and how they should be embodied within design pedagogy are defined. The final section of this chapter discusses 'Teaching Technological Knowledge'. It begins by acknowledging that technological knowledge that cannot be expressed in propositions must be taught using different strategies to oral instructions and textbooks. Learning by doing following the manner of the medieval guilds is suggested. It states:

> 'Pictures can play a supportive role here. Pictures are not propositions and they may be a useful complement in the process of oral instruction and demonstrating the skills'. (ibid: 47)

Although this is true, we would argue that pictures are rather more important than this implies and, as noted earlier, de Vries agrees that some images can embody design knowledge in themselves. As such 'images' would serve a similar role in design epistemology to 'propositions' for the traditional philosopher.

It goes on to discuss the need for teaching and learning to include the normative aspects of judging and assessing, and interdisciplinarity which:

> 'Some educationalists used to defend the thesis that technology should never be taught and learnt as a separate subject or course. But this does not do justice to the fact that technological knowledge is of a distinct kind …' (ibid: 48)

So, all-in-all, whilst the philosophy of technology can help to make a parallel case for the importance and distinctiveness of design epistemology, and assist with the identification of some of the kinds of knowledge required, there is seemingly little to be found concerning the forms of design knowledge and appropriate design pedagogy, and perhaps unsurprisingly.

Conclusion

We hope this publication will lead to a revival of interest in linking the theory, practice and teaching of design. It is not our intention simply to contribute a philosophical justification for design as an academically respectable subject. Our conviction is that any work on design epistemology should be founded in, and be useful to practitioners, educators, clients, policy makers and users. We are also acutely aware that in their everyday lives, everybody is an 'ordinary' designer shaping a personal, made environment. Many of the most acute problems facing contemporary society have a design aspect while the values and attitudes of consumer society place huge pressures on anyone engaging in design activity at any level.

We argue, therefore, that any attempt at an effective design epistemology should itself be designed as a framework which will help anyone – specialist and non-specialist alike – better understand the nature of design, its human significance and values. In particular, it should aim to increase the 'fluency' with which design is carried out, put into practice and evaluated. It should help us capture and learn lessons from the successes and failures of design activity and help in the teaching and learning of design.

This publication was always intended to be about agenda setting. It is not so much seeking to resolve the issues and difficulties surrounding the articulation of design epistemology, but to help to establish a framework within which they can be explored. It was also not intended to provide this framework by itself, but to serve as background reading for seminars that can develop it further. We would hope that such seminars could be organized at the institutions of our contributors, but also elsewhere. We would also hope that we could be present at some of these, either virtually or in reality. And so in order to provide a provisional framework for these seminars we have noted what seem to us to be key matters for discussion.

- Design epistemology needs to be articulated in terms of means not ends. Stating aspirational aims and objectives for design education adds very little to the debate. It is how designers achieve these aims and objectives that is the essential matter. What do they know? What forms does design knowledge take? What can they do? Design curriculum documents are rather better at stating aims and objectives than they are at stating the key matters of content.

- Design epistemology must engage with the interaction of material and ideological worlds. The intention of design activity is to support the survival of Homo Sapiens and the further development of humanity's cognitive abilities. Design operates in the area where the physical environment interacts with and influences the cultural/mental environment of 'institutional facts' and is determined by technology, social and personal beliefs and aesthetic perceptions.

- Design epistemology must engage with visual representations, which have been found to be central to design activity. Articulation of design activity in numbers, language and symbol systems are all important and have visual elements. However images can also represent and create design meaning and embody knowledge. It is as important, if not more important to engage with graphicacy, alongside numeracy and literacy.

- Curricula for design in general education must reflect these aspects of design epistemology and not become unduly influenced by the special pleading from particular design areas. Curricula for design in higher education are likely to be vocational and reflect particular design areas, although this is not, of course, inevitable.

- As research emerges in such fields as neuroscience and visual thinking, the role of images in the making of meaning and designing needs to be continually updated, and the implications for design epistemology and pedagogy understood and implemented.

LDP will be pleased to publish any contributions to furthering this agenda or addressing it, either through the Blog on LDP's website or with further publications as appropriate.

References

Blomberg (2010), *http://www.businessweek.com/innovate/di_special/20090930design_thinking.htm*

Department for Education, (2011). *The Framework for the National Curriculum. A report by the Expert Panel for the National Curriculum review*. Department for Education, London:

de Vries M J (2005) *Teaching About Technology: an introduction to the philosophy of technology for non-philosophers*, Springer, Dordrecht

Norman E (1998), 'The nature of technology for design', *International Journal of Technology and Design Education*, 67-87

AUTHOR PROFILES

Stephanie Atkinson
Stephanie Atkinson is a Professor of Design and Technology Education at the University of Sunderland. She has undergraduate qualifications as a Product and Furniture Designer from Northumbria University and a PhD from Newcastle-upon-Tyne University. Stephanie has held senior appointments in design and technology at all levels: in schools as Head of 3D Studies, as lecturer at Loughborough University and as Principal Lecturer, Reader and now Professor at University of Sunderland. Her early research for her PhD focused on the de-motivation of pupils in schools, but more recently she has been investigating the design activity of students training to become teachers in terms of designing styles and the relationship between such factors as learning styles, creativity, gender and computer aided learning, with many international publications to her name. She is a member of three international journal's editorial boards, examines PhD's internationally, is an external examiner for several universities and is the external advisor for Design and Technology for the International Baccalaureate Organisation and Edexcel. She has made an outstanding contribution as a teacher, teacher educator and researcher. Stephanie is widely respected within both design and educational fields. This was both recognised, and demonstrated, by her invitations to present keynote lectures. Firstly in 2009 to all design and technology teachers, inspectors and teacher trainers in Cyprus and again in 2009, the John Eggleston Memorial Lecture at the Design and Technology Association's International conference followed by the International Education Technology Education Conference (TERC2012) at Griffith University in Australia in 2012. In 2010 the Design and Technology Association presented her with an award for 'Outstanding Contribution to Design and Technology Education' and in 2011 she was awarded an MBE in the Queen's Birthday Honours for services to Higher Education.
stephanie.atkinson@sunderland.ac.uk

Ken Baynes
Ken Baynes' initial education was as a stained glass designer at a rural art school in Devon and the Royal College of Art in London. However, he has spent his professional career working as a designer, cultural historian and advocate of design education. At the centre of his work, have been two main themes: the use of exhibitions as a medium for education and entertainment and the attempt to develop better strategies for teaching art and design. He was Head of the Design Education Unit at the Royal College of Art and was a Visiting Professor at the Loughborough Design School. Working with the Welsh Arts Council he developed a series of pioneering exhibitions that explored the relationship between art and society. With his wife Krysia he has specialized in exhibitions that appeal to children and family groups and which emphasize making and aesthetic awareness. They have been shown in London, Scandinavia, Edinburgh, Glasgow and the United States. He worked with Malachite to research and present two television series on design for Channel 4. His books include About Design, Art in Society and (with Francis Pugh) *The Art of the Engineer*.
ken@ldpress.co.uk

Xenia Danos

Xenia is an expert in education with a passion for the areas of learning and development. Throughout her career she has experienced the learning and development process from different angles. As a secondary teacher, she witnessed the positive transformation of (often labelled as the troublemakers or weak) students, who would become inspired individuals with the need to set and achieve life goals. She soon realised that as a teacher, she had very little power to change the school system and was also intrigued in understanding the patterns which she had witnessed. This led her to do a PhD in human cognitive development (i.e. learning and teaching) with regards to visual intelligence – focusing on how humans learn and how new knowledge is constructed. She has been working on learning and development ever since, teaching, coaching and mentoring people as young as 10 all the way to 80+ years of age. Over the past 5 years, she has worked on various EU funded research projects, focusing on teaching and learning pedagogies, problem solving competences, creativity competences and formative and summative feedback and assessment. She is continuing her quest for learning and development, and she is currently working as the education officer and research coordinator in a Vocational Education Training centre.
xdanoskes@gmail.com

Alison Hardy

Alison Hardy is a senior lecturer at the Nottingham Institute of Education, part of Nottingham Trent University (NTU). She has been involved in design and technology education since 1993, as a teacher, head of department, mentor for student teachers and teacher educator. Since joining has NTU she has been an External Examiner for undergraduate and postgraduate programmes. She also worked in further education where she was responsible for curriculum development and as an overseas lecturer at the University of West Bohemia in the Czech Republic. Currently completing her PhD, *The value of a school subject: Investigating the values attributed to design and technology by different stakeholders*, Alison has spent time exploring the influences and origins of the values we attribute to D&T. She is also a Trustee for the Design and Technology Association and in 2015 she was recognised by the Association for her outstanding contribution to D&T.
alison.hardy@ntu.ac.uk

Steve Keirl

Steve Keirl is Reader in Design Education at Goldsmiths, University of London. He has worked in Design and Technology (D&T) teacher education, in-service and postgraduate teaching and research in universities in Australia and the UK since 1994. He is a Design and Technology curriculum theorist with interests in national and international curriculum development. His research explores the relationships amongst ethics, curriculum, pedagogy, democracy, design, and technology – loosely seen as 'explorations of Technological and Design Literacy'.

He has published over 70 peer-reviewed papers and chapters and has led numerous education forums and workshops, conducted consultancies, and has given invited papers and keynote addresses, both nationally and internationally. In Australia, he chaired the

Technology Expert Working Group and was principal writer for the D&T Learning Area of the South Australian Curriculum Framework. In this he was instrumental in introducing the curriculum innovation of Critiquing as a key strand of D&T Education for all children. He was also a key researcher in national and international studies investigating Technology Education in Australian Schools and is a referee for several international D&T conferences and journals.
S.Keirl@gold.ac.uk

Graham Newman
Graham comes from a graphic design and film making background. Graham's focus is on design practice in research, specialising in design for social innovation, technology, strategy and design education. He is currently studying at the Royal College of Art as an MRes RCA Communication Design candidate. Graham has been a practicing designer for 25 years, fifteen of which are in Hong Kong. His early career included working in the design studio for Factory Records and the Haçienda nightclub in Manchester UK.

Most recently, he was a Design Manager at Li and Fung. Graham is a Director of Liberty Asia which provides new solutions to change the way slavery and trafficking is addressed by leveraging technology available to the corporate sector and providing it to NGOs.
graham.newman@network.rca.ac.uk

Eddie Norman
Eddie Norman is Emeritus Professor of Design Education at Loughborough Design School (LDS), UK. His research concerns the relationship of technologies and designing in relation to general and higher education, and associated pedagogical issues. He was leader of the Design Education Research Group, published widely and supervised 7 PhD students. He contributed to teaching at LDS on undergraduate and masters design programmes. He has been an External Examiner for undergraduate and masters programmes and PhD research submissions (eg Bath Spa, Brunel, Goldsmiths, NIE Singapore and the University of Limerick). He was Editor of *Design and Technology Education: an international journal* from 2005-2015 and has recently founded the specialist publisher Loughborough Design Press Ltd with Ken Baynes. Prior to joining LDS he had careers both in secondary education and as a profsesional engineer.
eddie@ldpress.co.uk

Tristram Shepard
Tristram Shepard studied Industrial Design before becoming a secondary school Head of Art, Design and Technology. He then became a freelance educational and publishing consultant and was the series editor of 'Design&Make It!' and 'Getting IT Right' for Nelson Thornes. During this time Tristram was also an Ofsted inspection team member for Art and Design and Technology. More recently he has worked with the Goldsmith's TERU team on various projects, including the e-scape e-portfolio initiative, and currently runs Design Direct Learning, an online publishing website.
tristramsipad@f2s.com

David Spendlove
David Spendlove is Professor of Education at the University of Manchester and is a member of numerous local, national and international strategic boards and is a member of two international editorial boards. He has an extensive list of publications and has presented at a large number of national and international conferences on a range of subjects.

David's research interests are diverse but are primarily located around curriculum, pedagogy and teacher development. In 2013 he received an 'Outstanding Contribution Award' from the Design and Technology Association, their highest accolade, and he is currently head of initial teacher education overseeing a number of high quality programmes providing different routes into teaching.

Most recently David has worked with colleagues at Kings College and other universities developing Teacher Development 3.0, examining how we create a sustainable high quality teaching culture. He is also currently researching teacher stress, design thinking and the context and unique contribution of universities to teacher development.
david.spendlove@manchester.ac.uk

Also available from Loughborough Design Press ...

DESIGN EDUCATION: A Vision for the Future
Edited by Ken Baynes and Eddie Norman

Developing a modern, progressive design education curriculum ... a book for politicians, manufacturers, business people, school governors, headteachers, interested parents and other policymakers.

Published in 2013, this book contributed to the review of design in general education in England and provides a framework for deeper reflection on future curricula. Still just as relevant today:

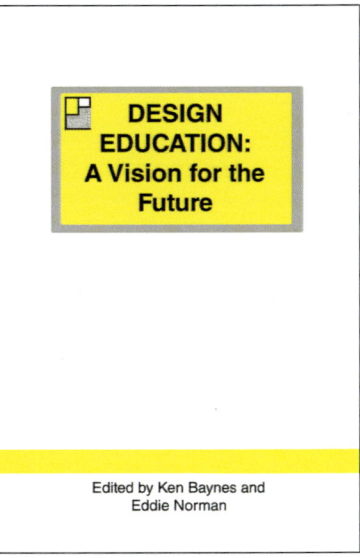

Christopher Frayling has written a Foreword

Ken Baynes & Eddie Norman have put forward Recommendations

Phil Roberts provides a means to review and develop curricular provision and practice

Eddie Norman provides an overview of research in design education

And for future reflection ...

In 2010 Ken Baynes gave the John Eggleston Memorial Lecture at the Design and Technology Association's Education and International Research Conference. He proposed 7 Key Themes that should be considered in developing design education curricula. In this book Ken revisits these themes and leading design education academics have joined forces to contribute further to their discussion.

Phil Roberts ... The Aims of Design Education

Eddie Norman & Ken Baynes ... The Significance of Practical Education

Stephanie Atkinson ... Encouraging the Imagination

Krysia Brochocka & Ken Baynes ... The Cognitive Value of Aesthetic Awareness

Giil Hope ... The Value of Learning Through Making

Niall Seery & Eddie Norman ... The Creative Relationships between Designing and Making

Eileen Adams ... The Educational Purpose of Doing Design Projects